BRANDING
SPEED

FRITZ WILKE

Copyright © 2021 by Fritz Wilke

The events and conversations in this book have been set down to the best of the author's ability. Some names and identifying details have been changed to protect the privacy of individuals.

All rights reserved. No part of this book may be reproduced or used in any manner without written permission of the copyright owner except for the use of quotations in a book review. For more information, email fritz@fritzwilke.com.

First paperback edition August 2021

Cover and book design by Steve Kuhn of
KUHN Design Group—KuhnDesignGroup.com

Front cover photograph courtesy of Rick Corwine—
find more of his work at RickCorwine.smugmug.com

Additional photography credits on page 227.

ISBN Paperback 9798462210570

Learn more about the author at fritzwilke.com

For Kristine and Will.

Thank you for putting up with me being gone so often to pursue my racing dreams, for understanding my self-imposed deadlines, and for putting up with my constant questions about colors, shirt styles, liveries, and our growing collection of FWR, Flying Ghost, and Ollie Rocket merchandise. Thank you for letting me do this and letting me be me.

BRANDING
SPEED

HOW TO MARKET YOUR CLUB RACING TEAM AND CREATE THE IMAGE YOU WANT

FRITZ WILKE

CONTENTS

Introduction　9

PART I: BRANDING PRINCIPLES

1. What is Branding?　15
2. Building Your Brand Purpose　27
3. Building Brand Character　37
4. Building Brand Goals　47
5. Finding Your Brand Voice　59
6. Your Brand Personality　71
7. Building Brand Consistency　81

PART II: HOW TO APPLY BRANDING TO YOU AND YOUR RACING TEAM

8. Team Names　93
9. Logos　103
10. The Race Car and the Racing Driver　117
11. Personal Brand and Racing Team Brand　127
12. Building Your Branded Gear Store　137

PART III: BUILD YOUR RACING BRAND ONLINE

13. Generating Content　151
14. Choosing Online Options　165
15. Social Media Posting Schedules　175

PART IV: BUILDING PARTNERSHIPS

16. How to Find Partners   185
17. Embrace Product Partnerships   197
18. Using Your Brand to Open the Right Doors   207

Closing Thoughts   213
Reading List   217
Photography Resources   219
Fritz Wilke Racing Partners   221
The Next Step   223
Acknowledgements   225
Photography Credits   227
About the Author   229

INTRODUCTION

This book is a how-to, yes, but it's also a guide about how to think about marketing and branding and apply both to your race program. Above all, this book is a thank you to those who've helped us succeed. It is my way of giving back to the next generation of racers growing into this sport that we love.

No matter what stage you compete on—club road racing, drag racing, dirt and paved oval, rally, off-road, karting—the marketing principles remain the same.

Branding is social. It's mainstream marketing. It's taking unusual steps and delivering a level of professionalism rarely seen on the club side of things. Being a good marketer is about understanding your potential partner's needs. In this book, I'll cover branding and brand marketing along with case studies and our own disasters and successes.

I'll show you exactly what we've found to work for our teams—Fritz Wilke Racing, Ollie Rocket Racing, and Flying Ghost Racing—and what did not. I'll reveal what you need to stand out from the crowd and how to be memorable. I'll help you learn what you need to get noticed. I'll give you the tools that can, with hard work and determination, open the right doors.

So how did I get here? To this point? To sitting down to write this book?

I lost my job, that's how.

I worked as a marketer for Ford for 12 years. In May of 2019, I started my third year in what would be my last job at Ford. It was a job I loved, working with the people at Ford who get it—the mad monk squad of men and women who make up Ford Performance. I was lucky enough to work on many Ford Performance projects during that time, including the Ford GT. In the downsizing that came in 2019, I was let go.

In my career, I worked in brand, product, event and performance marketing, strategy, and more. I started in 2006, working on what would later become the Fiesta ST. I was Mustang Brand Manager from 2008 to 2011 and helped supervise the marketing launches of the 2009–2011 Mustangs and the pre-launch of the 2012 Boss 302. I was also Ford's Performance and Enthusiast Event Manager, responsible for the creation and operation of Ford Enthusiast displays at Barrett-Jackson Auto Auctions, Shelby Events, the 45th Anniversary of Mustang, and NASCAR. I worked on car guy programs, was a part of Team Mustang, helped launch a billion-dollar brand in Asia, and helped bring Mustang to Australia!

At Ford, I had the blessing and curse of being a car guy.

The blessing was that I knew and loved history, so I could use ideas from the past and look at them with fresh eyes. That keen understanding of automotive history came in handy as we sought relevance with our performance enthusiasts. Credibility was the rock I broke ideas against for our enthusiast displays. Any idea or public presentation of the Mustang brand had to be credible to our Mustang enthusiasts. No matter how cool we or anybody else thought an idea was, if our enthusiasts thought it was lame, we weren't doing it. We used to say Team Mustang was always moving forward, but never forgot our past.

The curse side was subtler.

I know enthusiasts. I know enthusiasts from all walks of the automotive spectrum. I crewed for a late model team when I was in middle and high school, and I worked for John Buffum's Hyundai Rally Team after college. My German teacher was a friend of the Porsche family. Friends of our family collected Indy Cars. I had friends who street raced in the 90s. I had friends who were Honda guys and VW guys before that. I'm a race fan who also autocrossed, road raced, rallied, and ice raced. I was a service manager at an Acura dealership in the middle of the 90s Honda and Acura performance craze. I'd seen a lot of automotive culture and met a lot of automotive enthusiasts before I'd ever set foot inside Ford Motor Company.

This meant that there were times I had a gut feel about an idea because I'd seen a version of it fail or succeed from an enthusiast's perspective in a different venue. With this real-world experience, I wasn't as data-driven as maybe I could have been. For some people, data is the only thing that matters; for others, it's a combination. I've always been a gut plus data kind of person.

I wasn't always right, but with the enthusiasts, I nailed it more often than not. Like when we brought Vaughn Gittin, Jr. and his drift show to the vintage events at Road America. Part of the draw of vintage events is seeing cars sliding through the corners. That's exactly what drifting delivers. The fans loved it!

For most of my career, I worked on projects I was passionate about. I had a lot of great mentors to thank for making me the driven marketer that I am today. Robert Parker, Theo Benson, Vivian Palmer, Paul Anderson, Jim Farley, and Mark Fields all helped me understand what it means to be a marketer.

My enthusiasm for cars, car culture, and racing developed pretty early. I remember my dad listening to the Indy 500 every Memorial Day Weekend on the radio in the garage in Northwest Indiana. In the winter, he took my brothers and me up to the Chicago Auto Show. I always made a beeline for the race cars and concept cars on display.

It was my dad who instilled in me this fantastic combination of curiosity, and passion for knowledge and science early on. This led to my interest in racing, cars, history, and reading that prompted me to pursue a career in automotive journalism. More than anything, I wanted to write about racing. Racing tugged at my soul. I got up early to watch F1 and watched the Silver Crown series on Thursday Night Thunder from right there in Indiana. Basically, any race that was on TV, I was watching.

The sound, the competition... if you've picked up this book, you know what it is that hooked you. For me, it was all of those things: history, legacy, competition, race craft, surviving the near ones, all of it. It's a different combination for each of us in this sport.

All of this reminds me how much I needed a book like this when I first started in club racing. I had no idea how to approach partners and sponsors. Certainly, the skeptical side of me didn't believe that a sticker on the side of my little SCCA club racing ITC Honda Civic was worth anything. It wasn't at the time, but not for the reasons I thought. More about that later.

When I started, I made the classic marketer-to-be mistake: I didn't take the time to know and understand my customers, my potential partners. In one Esponsor/partner meeting, without asking what they needed, I launched into what I could do for them. At the end, to a strangely quiet room, I asked for the close. Turns out that what I proposed to do for them wasn't at all what they wanted from me.

I assumed I knew why they were talking to me. If I'd taken the time to ask, I would have learned—as I did much later—that I totally could have done what they were looking for. Instead, I made a classic marketing mistake. I didn't take the time to know my audience. One simple question could have changed the course of the conversation. It was a painful mistake, but good learning. I find that I learn far more from my mistakes than from my successes.

In this book, I'll talk about what to say and how to approach potential sponsors, but what I most want to talk about is a mindset. I want you to think about yourself, your race team, and the way you present yourself in a way that instills confidence in the people you are connecting with. You will be judged based on how you present yourself by pretty much anyone you come across as a club racer: fans, friends, colleagues, corner workers, sponsors, interviewers, race officials, PR people. They all can become advocates for you.

You'll also learn how to put yourself in your sponsor's shoes and understand their perspective long before you set foot in their office. You'll know your audience and learn about who you're going to meet beforehand.

Building a strong brand takes a little time, a little marketing knowledge and experience, an understanding of your specific audience, and a keen knowledge of yourself. It seems simple, but knowing yourself can be one of the hardest topics we'll explore in this book.

Personal branding is a theme you'll see me come back to time and time again. Or, "You be You", as Mr. Robinson, my son's second-grade teacher, taught him. As long as you're true to yourself, your on-stage personality will be easy to assume.

Now it's time to dive in and start building your racing brand. Let's get going!

Fritz Wilke
Chelsea, Michigan—Fall 2020

PART I

BRANDING PRINCIPLES

1

WHAT IS BRANDING?

It's 1992 and I've just moved to Minneapolis after graduating from Drake University.

I didn't know anyone but my girlfriend. I was trying to find a way into racing. I had very little money, and I discovered that autocross was an inexpensive way into the sport. I could use a car I already had, entry fees were $20, and it was just show up and run.

At my first event, I met Mark and Mary Utecht and their great group of friends. Mark and Mary were autocrossing their Dodge Omni GLH-S (*Goes Like Hell, S'more*).

I soon learned Mark and Mary ran Mayhem Racing—a great team name! Back in 1992, Mayhem Racing was a club road racing team. They fielded a road racing Dodge Omni in the Sports Car Club of America's (SCCA) Improved Touring B (ITB) class for Mark. He was a multi-time Central Division and Land O' Lakes Region Champion in SCCA. Alongside Mark, Tom Schabel ran an identically prepared Ford Fiesta in Improved Touring C (ITC). The SCCA classes cars by speed. In the Improved Touring Class, ITA was fastest, ITB was the middle, and ITC was the slowest.

Mark's personal brand prioritized doing what's right followed closely by his driving talent, fierce competitiveness, and keen mechanical knowledge. He cut his teeth as a service station technician during college, so he'd seen and repaired just about everything. This experience came in super handy when things went wrong. Mark was always the first one to dive in and figure out how to get back on track.

He's a larger-than-life character who brings fun with him wherever he goes. Mark's personal brand drove the personality of Mayhem Racing. One of the things Mark said to me early on is that once the race car goes out onto the track, consider it lost; whatever you bring back is a bonus. There are no certainties in racing. Mark's fierce, competitive spirit was always there.

One of the first things I noticed about Mayhem Racing was the consistency of the car and the team's preparation. When I joined, there was the Ford Fiesta and Dodge Omni. Both were painted in the same refrigerator white with black lettering in the same font and large NASCAR-style numbers on the doors. Everybody on the team knew each other well and had a similar sense of humor, giving each other grief and laughing often.

I helped at several events in 1992 and got to know everybody during autocrosses and subsequent Minnesota Autocross Club meetings. In the summer of 1992, I crewed for Mark and the team up at Brainerd International Raceway. We raced hard during the day on Saturday, ate well, and sat around the campfire telling stories until late at night, only to be up early and doing it all over again on Sunday.

Mayhem Racing was the first branded road racing team I was a part of, and it was the team that shaped my racing experience for years to come.

FROM PERCEPTION TO REALITY

First and foremost, this is a book by a club racer for club racers. With this as my focus, I want to avoid a boring textbook definition of branding wordsmithed by a dozen staffers. For us racers, branding is about giving our audience, partners, and fans a reason to choose us over our competitors.

You and your club team are either actively or passively branding yourself with each action, each event, each social media post, and each fan interaction.

Branding is much more than your logo or paint scheme, though these are important elements of every good club racing brand. A brand is made up of character and voice, trust and consistency, and so much more.

As I thought about how to define branding for us as club racers and club team owners, I kept coming back to creating and managing impressions. Just as marketing takes sales to the next level, branding takes marketing to the next level. Back in 1992, I understood Mayhem Racing's brand right away. It was clear to me the crew had a purpose: have fun winning.

So, let's dive into a little background on branding in racing. Individual and team branding has been around for a long time. From the beginning, drivers and teams sought to differentiate themselves.

In 1900, at the inaugural Gordon Bennett Cup, teams from four nations raced from Paris to Lyon. To help spectators identify each team's nationality, Count Elliott Zborowski, an American racing driver, introduced the idea of using country colors.

France would be in blue, and Belgium in yellow. White was assigned to Germany and red to the United States. Over the next few years, as more countries joined the race for the Bennett Cup, each was assigned, or chose, its own color. The list grew to include Britain, Austria, Switzerland, and Italy. When Britain joined in 1902, its national colors of red, white, and blue were taken, so the country adopted a shade of green reminiscent of the olive green on British locomotives, later to be known as British Racing Green.

Not long after the first Bennett Cup, Henry Ford secured the future of his Ford Motor Company with a famous win in his own car, *Sweepstakes*, over Alexander Winton in *Bullet*. A little later, the *Marmon Wasp* won at Indianapolis.

Country colors soon evolved to represent the nationality of the team. When Prince Scipioni Borghese of Italy won the 1907 Peking (Beijing) to Paris race in a bright red Fiat, Italy adopted Rosso Corsa or Racing Red as its national racing color in his honor. Italian car brands have competed in red ever since.

In the interwar period, the German national color changed to silver as the AutoUnion and later the Mercedes teams ran bare silver bodywork to save weight. From then on, the Mercedes teams would be known as the Silver Arrows. Those country colors were a convenient shorthand for entrants and fans alike. In essence, these ironic colors were each country's brand.

By the 1960s, the colors of the cars primarily reflected each team's nationality, but, as the sponsorship era dawned, car and team colors began to reflect brand partnerships.

Since then, branding has blossomed in motorsports. Every year, we see pro teams launching new brands and re-upping the mainstays in the sport. Racing, as you well know, has become so expensive at nearly every level that sponsor partnerships are often the main means of support for teams and drivers. Here's an example of a team building upon a positive initial impression to create a legendary brand.

FORD RAPTOR

Before the 2010 F-150 Raptor was launched, the market had never seen a vehicle branded as Raptor. It was an unknown. Raptor had multiple meanings—dinosaur, bird of prey. In this case, it was never purposefully defined, letting consumers own part of the new brand.

Raptor's first task, after wowing the crowd at SEMA, was to run the 2008 Baja 1000. It finished the race and the impression of the Raptor as a super-capable, off-road-focused, desert pre-runner-style truck was born. The SEMA truck's Baja 1000 finish built the foundation of the Raptor brand.

Ford and SVT, now Ford Performance, have strengthened the Raptor's brand perception with each successive generation.

Raptor worked because the imagery was right and the truck was outstanding. Could we have called it Maverick? Probably. As long as the brand name wasn't obviously lame, the perception would have stuck. The brand name becomes tied to the perception of the product.

MARLBORO, DUPONT, CASTROL

The elements of our club racing branding, while consistent with branding in general, are tailored specifically for our niche. Each element has its own impact on how we drive the perception of ourselves, our team, and our racing.

In club racing, branding is important on and off track. We will use branding to set ourselves apart from our competitors. Sometimes in racing, the brand is more memorable than the week-to-week results. You still have to perform on track, but a strong brand makes a top five finish stronger and is more memorable among fans and partners alike.

We're going to go into detail on what a strong and well-managed brand can do for you and your team and what you can do to cultivate and grow your brand. We'll also look at how a weak or inconsistent brand can hold you back and make you invisible.

In essence, our club racing branding is a form of shorthand. Whether we're go karting, drag racing, or racing sports cars or motorcycles, our own branding is a shorthand. Think of the Marlboro McLarens, the Dupont Chevy, and the John Force Castrol Funny Cars. These brands deliver a consistent image. The great brands in racing, parts stores, race tracks, and teams all build their brands on consistency, familiarity, and trust. They provide us a memorable shorthand.

You know what you're getting when you cheer for a driver brand or a team brand. You know who you're cheering for and the rest fall into obscurity. These impressions are a result of a series of brand elements that build from brand purpose to brand consistency.

We're working up to a definition of branding that will guide us throughout this book and will help us develop and grow our individual and team brands. So, as I seek to define branding and help you understand how marketing and branding can help all of us club racers, I need to make sure you and I are speaking the same language. The language of both marketing and branding. Consumer perception drives the reality of brands. Always. For good or bad, consumer perception will become reality.

So, as I think about our club racing brand as a shorthand, I keep coming back to a brand as a promise. In its simplest form, our brand promise is delivered through impressions.

When I talk about impressions, these are not impressions as defined by social media companies. Social media defines impressions as content seen for a certain number of seconds on a newsfeed scrolled through on a phone or computer.

While social media can generate impressions for sure, the impressions I am talking about here are the ones formed by real-life interactions with specific brands. These are the impressions we as club racers have the most control over. It is critical for us to manage the impressions we create as we build and grow both our personal and team brands.

How do you want to be known as a racer? Do you race fair, but hard? Are you sneaky? How far do you bend the rules? When you're out there racing, it's important to be true to yourself. Be aware of how people will talk about you and the impression you make.

This right here is the essence of branding for us as racers. We brand ourselves and, through our branding, we manage the impressions others have of us. Most of the time, we don't even know it; we're just being ourselves.

We racers are all on stage—in the paddock, while talking with competitors, on the track, in victory circle, in impound, on the way home, and on social media. All of these on-stage moments are an opportunity to be true to your brand, to build your brand—or not. Once we recognize that we get to choose how we represent ourselves, our branding becomes a powerful tool.

Think of your interactions with your favorite local businesses. Finish these sentences:

I love going there. They always…

I like them because they…

The answers you thought of are likely the result of a business owner's careful guidance to deliver a specific and unique brand promise.

EMBRACE YOUR EGO

Racing is a sport where the team is just as important as the individual competitor. How do we separate the individual and the team and how do we separate the person from the personal brand? As you build your brand, consider the interaction between you, your team, and your personal brand.

So, how are team and personal brands different? First and foremost, recognize you are your own brand. Your personality, your experiences, your history, and your successes and failures are all part of your personal brand. I have found that the core of your personal brand is absolutely true to your beliefs, your passions, and your experiences.

Your personal brand is often you, but just a little bit better or a little bit more. You hear it so many times about meeting a larger-than-life personality—they were so similar in real life to the personality seen on TV. It's difficult to craft a personal brand that diverges from your natural personality. Most of us club racers are just us, take us or leave us. We're not playing games with our on-stage personalities. We've got way too much to do during a race weekend to assume a persona or personality that is out of character.

However, as any of you who have spoken on stage have experienced, there is a side of you as a club racer that's a little bigger than what you typically show the people around you. For some of us, when we get in the race car, on the bike, or in the go kart, we become slightly more than we are in the paddock. Call it ego. Sure, we racers all have an ego. Ask your significant other. Our ego is a tool we can use as we enhance our personal brand.

Lots of people do this via social media now. We've all seen the profiles of people who only post their awesomeness or adventures, or those who only post negativity. Think of those social media posts when considering your ego on the track—there's you, and the best version of you.

As you build and enhance your personal brand, please make sure you *can* live up to it and actually *want* to live up to it. As you build your personal brand, it may be tempting to try to become larger than life. If that's not you, people will see right through it. Instead of benefiting you, it will become a strike against you.

Your personal brand is going to be the one your fans identify with and come to expect, so it should be easy for you to slip into. Often, you'll enhance your personal brand by being as intensely true to yourself as you can be. This is not about smoke and mirrors. This is about you being you.

Really. Just be yourself here.

As you think about how you want to create your personal brand, consider the elements of your personality that you want to emphasize. Do you have a dry wit? Are you super intense or are you soft spoken? Do you feel like the ultimate underdog? Are you resilient?

Any of these qualities can be something to expand. We all have different aspects of our personalities and we can choose which elements to showcase.

Just a quick note here on you as a person, you as a brand, and how your brand fits into a larger team. Your personality can help a team bloom or it can hold a team back. As club racers, our teams are often a group of friends who love to go to the track, race, make memories, and have a ton of fun in the process. We love racing in all its forms. It's why we spend so much time on it. When your personal brand and your team's brand complement each other, you build both brands without even thinking about it.

THE ELEMENTS OF BRANDING

This branding shorthand is built on a structure of branding elements, the foundation of our club racing branding. There are six key elements of branding, and each element is supported by the others. Together, they generate consistent, cohesive impressions for our audience of partners, fans, friends, and family who will then understand the shorthand for us and our club racing brand.

In the following chapters, I'll explore these elements individually and I'll show you how to own each of them. I'll show you how to bend a brand element to your individual will and use it to strengthen the whole of your brand. As you craft and refine your personal and team branding, you will find that it becomes easier and easier to focus on how to differentiate your brand from your competitors within your series.

These are the key elements of a racer and race team's brand:

1. Purpose—why you do what you do
2. Character—how you will achieve your goals
3. Goals—what you are trying to achieve
4. Voice—how you talk about what you're doing
5. Personality—how you breathe life into your brand
6. Consistency –how you build familiarity and trust

Brand Purpose. Your club racing brand starts with your brand purpose, the why. This is the reason you do what you do.

This first one is deceptively difficult. Take a moment to think about your purpose: why you do what you do in racing. For us as racers, we intuitively answer the question of why we race with "win races and championships." That reason isn't terribly differentiating from other racers when everybody wants to do the same. Apart from winning races and championships, why do you race? The answer to *that* question is going to be far more personal and interesting.

As practice, try to figure out the brand purpose, the why, for any corporation that comes to mind. Now, do it without answering "to make money" and it becomes a lot more difficult.

Often, for a brand purpose, I'll use the phrase "I believe" to generate that why element. This brand purpose starts off with why you race. It is intensely personal and can be anything that is true to you.

Some examples include:

I believe I can help others have fun racing.

I believe that I will become world champion.

I believe racing is a great escape from the everyday.

I believe in new experiences.

This brand purpose is intensely individual and usually takes the longest of all the elements to properly explain—even to yourself. It involves a bit of navel gazing to be sure, but it guides every step afterwards on the path to building a great club racing brand—whether it is for you or your team.

Brand Character. If your brand purpose is your why, your brand character is your how. Just like your purpose, your character guides your brand. How you fulfill your brand purpose is your brand character. Brand character is made up of things you will and won't do in pursuit of your purpose. It is your guiding light, your version of right and wrong, your answer to the shopping cart theory.

The shopping cart theory goes something like this—there is no inherent benefit to you for putting a shopping cart back where it goes. There is also no penalty for leaving it next to your car and driving away. No one is going to praise you for putting the cart back. No one is going to arrest you for leaving it behind. Only your own sense of right and wrong will determine whether you put the cart back. So the question is: Will you do the right thing when no one is watching?

Another example of character is a story about Michelangelo. He was working on the back of a statue intended to be placed high up in a church alcove. When asked why he didn't just skip the back and leave it rough as no one would know, he responded, "Because, I'll know."

Your brand character doesn't need to be all high and mighty, but it is the moral compass for your brand.

Brand Goals. So far, your brand knows why it exists and how it will act, so now it needs a goal. Your brand goal is the overarching target for your brand's mission, its reason for existing. Your brand goal is your roadmap to where your brand is and where you want your brand to be. Your brand goal is what others say about where you are going or what you are doing.

Brand Voice. This brings us to brand voice, which ties brand character and brand personality together. Brand voice is the way you communicate verbally, visually, in person, on track, and on social media. All of these should use a consistent and distinct voice. This brand voice sets the tone for your brand in all communications and helps others unfamiliar with your brand learn who you are.

Brand Personality. Your brand personality is who you want to be known as in the racing world. Are you intense, thoughtful, driven, funny, silly, or bigger than life? All of these characteristics feed into your brand personality and your team's brand personality. More than anything, your brand personality is the essence of you. We'll go into much more detail in the brand personality chapter, but this is one of the most fulfilling parts and often the easiest part of brand building as you're just being yourself.

However, don't get caught in the trap of wanting your brand to be something that you're not. If you aren't as outgoing as Ken Block or Vaughn Gittin, Jr., then I advise you not to build your personality like theirs. It is exhausting when you're trying to be something you're not.

This is your You be You. So, be true to yourself. If you're larger than life, be larger than life. If you're quietly driven, be quietly driven. More than anything, and I cannot stress this enough, you be you. People and potential partners can see through brands that talk the talk, but don't walk the walk.

So, understand why you do this crazy sport we all love. Embrace your brand purpose. Then, know how you're going to do it and live it and embody your brand character. Set your brand goals. Give your brand a voice and infuse it with personality.

Brand Consistency. To bring your brand together, you need to be consistent. This is the final step in building a brand and probably the hardest of all the elements to get right. The world is constantly changing and you'll feel constant pressure to change things up—your logo, your voice, your personality.

Consistency comes from nailing the first five brand elements and then committing to them. Your voice, your personality, your goals all support the purpose. The way you communicate and drive towards your brand goals reinforces your brand identity at each step.

Your brand consistency becomes a guiding light for your followers, and an easy shorthand for everything you do. Your brand creates an image in your followers and partner's minds. Think red Ferrari. The more consistent you make each element of your brand, the more memorable and powerful your brand will become.

This isn't to say that brands cannot change direction with changing times; however, there needs to be a substantial, compelling reason behind a change. This is more than moving up to a different series.

Think of a company that recently changed their logo and how that made you think of them. Why change now? What drove the change? Was their stated reason compelling enough?

Think of writing that same change statement for your brand. To rebrand or change direction is just like starting your brand over again. It can be done, but it typically loses a lot of the strength of the original.

You can change names, logos, colors, series, or drivers, but if you change the purpose, character, goals, voice, or personality of your brand, it is like moving a sports team to another city—a lot of your brand building will need to start over.

Again, changes aren't the end of the world, but know the hill you are going to climb and reflect back on your you be you to make sure you are being true to yourself in rebranding. Name changes and series changes aren't that big of a deal. In club racing, we're all looking to move up the ladder. You can take all the work you've put into your brand and move it up the ladder with you. I'll show you how.

Ok, on to the next bit. Let's explore the first and most important of the brand elements: brand purpose.

2

BUILDING YOUR
BRAND PURPOSE

It's 1978. I'm nine years old.

My dad asked me to come with him on an errand. I didn't really want to go, but I hopped in the car anyway. Little did I know that impromptu adventure would change my view of the world. We met with one of my dad's friends at his auto parts business. It was a normal parts store in front but, in back, they had a huge warehouse with a drive-up ramp to storage on the second level. Dad and I walked up the ramp and as we came level with the second floor, I saw wedge-shaped car after wedge-shaped car covered by dull gray canvas.

I saw race cars hiding their secrets under those dusty tarps—roadsters from the 50s, mid-engine cars from the late 60s and winged beasts from the 70s. I remember, clear as day (which likely means much of this is misremembered), seeing my first ChampCar up close and personal. It ran a few years before, perhaps in 1975. Dad left me up there to poke around and went back down to the store to chat with his friend.

As is often the case, the most poignant events of a child's life are missed by parents. I looked at each car, tentatively lifting each tarp by the corner to discover the wire wheels or aluminum wings hidden underneath. After a while, I began to get brave. I peeled the tarp back on one of the winged ChampCars.

After a long, internal debate about asking permission, I quietly slipped my thin nine-year-old frame into the driver's seat. I sat there, barely able to see out of the cockpit. I placed one hand on the gear lever off on the side sill to the right, one on the steering wheel, and tried to reach the pedals. I could, just barely.

The smell of the car was musty and old, sharp and slightly oily. I looked at the dials and gauges in front of me, not really knowing what they were for. The seat was padded vinyl all around me. I felt the history of the car. I closed my eyes and listened. In my head I could hear the announcers, the scream of the engines, the roar of the crowd at Indy. The car felt wrapped around me, sharp edges all covered by padding.

After a while I realized I had been lost in my imagination for a long time. All of a sudden, I was panicking, positive I was going to get in trouble. I needed to get out. I'm sure I stepped where I wasn't supposed to when I scrambled out. I listened. All I heard were normal warehouse sounds. Nobody was coming.

I relaxed a bit, looked around a little, and uncovered more cars. There were maybe 10 or 12 cars in all. The tall, skinny ones with huge steering wheels were Offy-Roadsters. The low, cigar-shaped ones were old, and the tires looked huge.

I only sat in one car that day, but it changed the course of my life and made a deep impression on me that has stayed with me ever since. I never told my dad about sitting in his friend's car. I didn't want to get in trouble and, in a way, it was my secret to keep.

Not long after that life-changing experience, my dad and I were in our garage at home. I watched while he worked on the family car. It was Memorial Day Weekend. We lived in Northwest Indiana and, like the rest of the state, the broadcast of the Indy 500 was tape delayed on TV the following day for us.

The radio broadcast was also delayed, but started right after the live finish. It was late in the day and Dad played the broadcast on the radio. I remember hearing the announcers and imagining the racers diving into turn one as they described. I was off in my dusty car from the warehouse, gripping the wheel, peering down the nose, and diving underneath my competitors in a blend of my imagination, Speed Racer, and the voices on the radio.

I stayed all day helping Dad, listening to the race on the old, solid state transistor radio, visions of race car drivers in my mind.

Those dusty smells and that scratchy radio broadcast still echo in my memory and remain a strong influence on me to this day. I didn't know it at the time, but those two events would shape my brand purpose and my direction.

PUT A BACKBONE IN YOUR BRAND

The brand purpose, the why, is the most important part of any brand. A strong brand purpose helps define your brand's foundation. It is your driving force, the reason you race.

If you're clear about your brand purpose, those who admire and identify with it will follow and cheer you on. A strong brand purpose helps potential partners see the real you. It helps them identify commonalities and search for ways to work together.

Your club racing brand purpose doesn't have to be overly emotional nonsense. It does have to be clear and it does have to be true to you. If it is both of these things, then it will become a roadmap for you. Your brand purpose will guide you in times of success and failure, in times of growth, and in times when you need to pause.

Your brand purpose puts a backbone in your brand. It supports and guides all of your branding efforts. One of my titles is Chief Storyteller for FWR. When I race, I go on an adventure for the weekend and bring back stories to share. It's those adventures and stories that drive my brand purpose—just like the adventure I had in that dusty old warehouse sitting in race cars all those years ago.

Here's an example of how brand purpose guides me. Each year, near the end of the season, we talk about what next year looks like for our team. Each year, we want to go to new tracks and have new adventures. Each year, we want to race new people from all over the country and create new stories. If, for instance, I wanted to race at the same track every weekend, this would be at odds with my own specific brand purpose as the adventure element of my brand purpose would suffer. The story element of my brand purpose wouldn't suffer as much, but it would be missing the travel portion of the adventure.

Brand purpose also guides what I share on social media. Adventure and stories are important to me and my brand, so these are the things I tend to share. With my brand purpose in front of me, I can focus on managing next steps and laying out the path for the following season.

Brand purpose is there to help guide you as you expand and grow, and will enhance your personal and team brands. It becomes your mission, your why.

Let's look at a couple of examples of corporate brand purposes: one strong and one weak.

Let's start with a hypothetical company that has a weak corporate purpose (I'm trying not to get myself in trouble here). Their corporate purpose is to make money, sell more stuff, and deliver value for their shareholders.

Why is this bad? Well, it's not very specific and has little to do with their industry. None of the purposes above are bad in and of themselves, but they need clarity. If your purpose is to make money, sell more stuff, and deliver value to shareholders, how do those criteria protect the business when an executive decides the company should jump into a completely unrelated market? If the company sells staplers and an executive sees a way to make money in tennis shoes, the brand purpose says they should do it.

However, if the brand purpose is holding the world together one great staple at a time, then that focus is present. You sell staplers, you sell great staplers, you build staplers to help customers solve their stapling needs. I'm laughing while typing this. Good Lord.

With this clear brand purpose, when the exec comes in with the shoe idea, you can measure it up against your mission and purpose and make an informed decision. You may still decide to sell tennis shoes, but maybe with another brand, not your "one great staple at a time" stapler brand.

Now, let's look at a company with a great brand purpose.

WARBY PARKER—DISRUPTING THE EYEGLASS INDUSTRY

Warby Parker was founded in 2010 by a group of business-school students commiserating about the high cost of glasses. This was at a time when a new pair of glasses cost $600—three times the price of a then-new iPhone 3G.

The founder, Dave Gilboa, lost a pair of glasses while traveling in Thailand and needed to replace them. He was talking with other business-school friends about it. One of the friends had worked at an eyeglass non-profit and had experience creating eyeglasses for less than $10 a frame.

They wondered why glasses were 60 times more expensive and what was causing it.

They researched the industry and realized a couple of major brands owned most of the market for eyeglasses. With this near-monopoly power, those two brands could effectively set pricing. And thus, the Warby Parker brand purpose of making eyewear more affordable was born.

Everything Warby Parker does now revolves around this brand purpose. It is behind their movement into sunglasses (eyewear), contacts (eyewear), accessories like cleaning kits and cases (for eyewear), and eye exams (for eyewear). The Warby Parker brand purpose is clear and guides them in a chaotic market with lots of potential for distraction. This clear brand purpose has made them the leading online retailer of eyeglasses.

I RACE BECAUSE...

So, what does this mean for us? Be simple, be focused, and be true to yourself. Simpler is always better here. But, as we're just getting started with this exercise, it's okay to start with a purpose that answers lots of anticipated questions. Then, you will need to thrift it down to become crystal clear.

Sometimes, when brainstorming, it's easier to thrift down to get clarity than it is to search for more to add. However, in this, be brief, be clear, and be simple. One sentence maximum. We'll get there, but this is your simple reason that your club racing brand exists. Remember: adventures and stories. Something like that.

For us club racers, our brand purpose should be, above all, honest to ourselves. Why do we race? Why do we follow our passions and spend our weekends at the track and our weeknights in the garage?

For some of us, we race to gain clarity or to find peace in the race car away from the distractions of the real world. For some, it's the speed and adrenaline, while for others, it's all about winning. Some like being cleverer than the next guy while others like being braver. For others still, it's the knowledge that preparation and perseverance deliver success.

Here are some ideas to get you thinking about your brand purpose. It has helped me when developing my brand purpose to use sentence starters like these: "Because I believe…", or "I race to…", or "I race because…"

Because I believe …

- racing makes me a better decision maker.
- I am a better thinker after racing.
- I can inspire others.
- I can help others learn to race.

I race to…

- spend time with friends.
- eliminate the distractions of everyday life and find peace.
- make memories with family.
- have fun at the racetrack.
- be the best at what I do.
- go fast and get that adrenaline rush.
- have adventures.
- see the world's great racetracks.

I race because…

- I love competition.
- I get to see friends.
- it's the only place where I can clear my mind and concentrate.
- I love winning.
- I love outsmarting the competition.
- I'm passionate about pushing the limits of what I can do.

As racers, each of our purposes is unique. Give it a go and see what rings true for you. Set this book down for a while and think about your own personal purpose. Think of why you race. It's tricky not to put goals in here like championships and wins per season, but don't. Save that for the next level up.

You're the only one reading your answer for now, so be as honest with yourself as you can. Take some time and really think this through. Now, write a few of them down on a piece of paper. These statements are the emotional reasons you race.

Okay, that was the hard bit. Now that we've sorted out ourselves, let's look at this from a team perspective. The purpose of a racing team may not be the same as the purpose of an individual racer. Again, it's easy to fall into the next level up goals answers here. Try to focus on the reasons for the existence of the team—the key answer to why we do this as a racing team.

Look at some of these examples that start off in a similar way with "We believe…" and "We …"

We believe…

- racing should be accessible to everyone.
- the best prepared car wins.
- anyone can race.
- racing can be competitive and fun.
- racing is fun first and everything else second.
- experiences are more important than things.
- adventures make us more interesting.

We…

- deliver unforgettable experiences.
- love the intensity of competition.
- build friendships.
- prove ourselves every day.
- see the world.
- have adventures.
- have fun at the track.

Each of these ideas gives us a distinct purpose and will guide us on our path towards brand building. When you lay out the personal and team branding purposes, you can see the connections and similarities and sometimes differences. It's important to understand how you and your team's branding can complement each other and where you might diverge.

If your main focus in racing is on competition and your team's focus is on having fun, you may not be able to get the help you need when you are in the thick of things. On the flipside, if you're focused on having fun and the team is focused primarily on competing, you may be pushing and pulling against each other from time to time.

LEAVE THE RIGHT IMPRESSION

So why have we spent so much time on writing down our purpose? It's because your brand purpose is the building block for every other element of your brand. Once you have your purpose, you can explore the how and what of your brand. Your purpose is the most differentiating piece of your brand. It's what makes you, you. This is the hardest thing you will do when building your brand.

If you get stuck, ask somebody close to you why they think you race, or why your team races. They may nail it, or they may be way off and when you speak to counter that misperception, listen to yourself speak. Your rebuttal is likely pretty close to the truth.

Both personal and team brands are built in similar ways. You already have a personal brand. You may not be amplifying it just yet, but you are unique. Your friends' impression of you, your co-workers' impression of you, the impression you leave with the server at a restaurant, the impression you leave with anyone you interact with—they are all part of your personal brand.

Some people know you well while some may not know your name, but the impression you leave after each interaction is a part of your personal brand. Think of your personal brand as your reputation. As a racer, your interactions and impressions matter to your personal brand and your reputation.

If you want to learn even more about brand purpose, Simon Sinek's book *Start with Why* is a phenomenal exploration of brand purpose. His Ted Talk is pretty amazing too.

Now we're ready to move on to our next element of a racer's brand: character.

3

BUILDING BRAND CHARACTER

It's 1994 and I'm racing the ITC Civic at Brainerd International Raceway.

It was the last race before the Divisional Runoffs at Putnam Park. We'd already won our season points championship and the car was a rocket. I led the race from the start and we were in the closing laps.

At the exit of turn six, I typically went wide onto some extra pavement on the other side of the curb. For one final time, just before I turned into six, I looked in my mirror and saw a much faster GT-5 car approaching out of five. I took my normal line and figured the other driver would catch me after the 7-8 chicane. He was a LOT faster than I thought and caught up to me at the exit of six while I was still outside on the extra pavement.

I assumed he was still behind me, so I came back on track to the left and promptly went across his nose onto the grass. My car spun backwards, dug in, and flipped end for end with a half roll for good measure. The car was in the air forever. There was a lot of quiet time. When the car finally came down, it landed flat on the driver's side. I hit my head hard on the sandy ground through the window net.

I climbed out and looked at the car. It was severely damaged, maybe destroyed. Less than two weeks to the Divisional Runoffs. Damn. I was furious with the other driver. Why had he hit me? Why? What the hell?

In the ambulance, I replayed the accident and it slowly dawned on me that it was my fault. Completely my fault. When I got out of medical, I tried to find the other driver, but he had already packed up and left. I never did get to talk to him about my mistake.

We had a wrecked car to fix. Some people would have given up and skipped the race in two weeks, but Mayhem Racing did not give up. Period. Persistence was part of our character. We knew we would get back on track. We found a new shell, swapped out the cage, the engine, and suspension, then had the car painted and lettered. The paint was still curing on the trailer!

At the Divisional Runoffs, I sat on pole, set a lap record, and won the race. It was a charmed weekend! Finishing that car in less than two weeks and winning with it at the next race was who we were as Mayhem Racing. All of it came out of our belief that no problem was too big to overcome. Crash damage, reliability issues, you name it, Mark and Mayhem Racing overcame it. It was part of Mayhem Racing's brand character.

That was an example of our brand character leading us towards success. Earlier in the year, I had the opposite experience when I let my team down by acting out of brand character. This was also at Brainerd. I was leading my class, trying to get by a slower car in a faster class. He was fast on the straights, but slow in the corners.

Brainerd has a long front straight followed by a pair of flat-out corners that lead to the 90-degree turn three. Turns four to nine have short straights between them that act as a rhythm section.

I would catch this driver at five or six and pass him. Then, he passed me on the long front straight before we did it all over again, lap after lap. Each lap, second place in my class was gaining on me. I finally got close enough to get by in three. I sat on his rear bumper and gave him a little nudge in the middle of the brake zone, dove under him, and made a big enough gap that he couldn't get by on the straight again.

I was celebrating with my team when that very same driver came up to me, angry. He poked his finger in my chest and told me how dangerous it was to bump him in the brake zone.

I prided myself on racing hard, but fair. In *his* mind, I was reckless and dangerous. I realized I had crossed the line.

I was suddenly embarrassed about how I had bragged to my crew about my clever move. I vowed never to do that on purpose again. I had spent a lot of time racing my way—fair, but hard—and the incident was out of character.

Over the years, that driver and I have come across each other in various roles. He's now a national race steward and he has this skeptical look in his eye when I say hi. As if to say, "I remember you."

If I had checked on him after the race, he still would have been mad, but the impression I left him with would have been different. Instead of being perceived as some arrogant kid who's willing to wreck anybody to get by, I could have at least offered an explanation.

Now, if I have contact on track, I seek out the driver involved after the race. I do it because I care about the people I race against. I care how I race and I care how people think I race. It's important to me to race clean, fair, and hard. It's part of my personal character and part of my brand character.

We're always making impressions, whether we realize it or not.

PUT THE SHOPPING CART BACK

So, you know why you do it. Now, how are you going to do it? Brand character comes down to one simple question: Who are you going to be known as?

When someone talks about you, what will they say? Will you do anything to win? How about wrecking the guy in front of you in the last corner? How about illegal parts on the car? How about clever interpretation of the rules?

This takes us back to the grocery cart example from earlier—what are you made of and what is your moral compass when it comes to club racing and your club racing team? This is about your actions on and off the track. It's hard to talk about brand character without getting all moralistic, but that's exactly the point—brand character is your brand's morals.

Character, more than anything, will define your brand's perception in the minds and eyes of others. Brand character isn't so much worrying about what others will think of you, but about being true to yourself and your vision for your brand. Brand character for us as club racers should come naturally. It should be the essence of your You be You. Your brand character is like your What Would [insert racer or team you admire] Do?

Brand character can be simple or super complex. Brand character takes a lot of work to maintain and it's easy to cut corners, but the real reward is when you do something truly out of your brand's character and somebody calls you out on it. When they say, "Wow, that wasn't like you," you'll know you've nailed the projection of your brand character.

FORD FLEX: THE URBAN, ANTI-MINIVAN

In 2008, Kate Pearce and Usha Ragavachari, the brand team that developed the brilliant marketing plan for the Ford Flex, had a challenge. The Flex was an upscale, uniquely designed, minivan-sized wagon. It was the minivan for those who would never drive a minivan. This predated the SUV craze of the 2010s. The Flex was so unique and so easily misinterpreted by mainstream Ford marketing that the brand team needed to guide the brand conversation from the beginning.

Kate and Usha believed that the Flex, positioned in urban, upscale territory, would succeed as an anti-minivan of sorts, but it would fail miserably should it be positioned as a direct minivan competitor and be forced to compete on price. The Flex was intended to be a lower-volume, premium-priced minivan alternative for hip parents who needed to be able to do the kid thing, but wanted an elegant solution.

On the surface, it seemed simple. Kate and Usha developed an "is/is not" list for their new, difficult-to-categorize vehicle. Their vision of the Flex's character was a series of comparison statements: "Flex is X, not Y. Flex is A not Z." And so on.

Flex was an urban activity vehicle. Yes, it could haul kids and soccer balls, but that wasn't its main purpose. Its main purpose was to be a stylish alternative to the mainstream minivan.

If a misinformed, but well-intentioned Ford marketer wrote copy or produced ads that were focused on the family or kids side of the equation, they were moving the Flex into a space where it was not equipped to compete. There were no sliding doors, no easily cleanable fabrics, no entry model, etc.

Family wasn't Flex's reason for existence. It could do the kid and family truckster thing exceptionally well, but that wasn't the focus of the Flex brand. The Flex team's "is/is not" list protected the Flex brand from mainstream Ford marketers. The list became an important part of a whole new theory of brand guidelines at Ford and its strength in protecting Flex successfully guided several generations of vehicle launches.

I WON'T MAKE IT EASY FOR THEM

As a club racer, our version of the list looks like this: I Will vs. I Won't. These statements about integrity and character speak to who we are and what we are willing to do. Exploring these will help us reveal our own brand character.

It's easy to get really grandiose here, but using a set of I Will and I Won't statements will help uncover truths about ourselves as a club racer and a club race team. The statement "I will do anything to win" is a little open ended and ominous. Will you wear the white hat or the black hat from Spy vs. Spy?

Here's a short bit of my list:

- I will give other competitors room
- I won't make it easy for them

- I will do my damndest to make clean passes
- I won't wreck people to get by

- I will check in on a competitor if we have contact
- I won't avoid the conversation

- I will make time for kids and fans in the paddock
- I won't avoid fans

- I will speak my mind
- I won't back down from confrontation

- I will look for an unfair advantage
- I won't blatantly cheat the rules

- I will drive a safe car
- I won't sacrifice safety for speed

- I will prepare for each race mentally and physically
- I won't blame lack of prep for lack of performance

- I will accept responsibility
- I won't avoid blame

- I will learn from my mistakes
- I won't avoid discussing them

My list above isn't for everybody. Some would say it's too nice, but that's a part of my brand character and who I am and the easiest character for me to stay true to. To populate your own list, think about situations you've found yourself in and how you handled yourself.

Be aware that this is the point when people sometimes go off the rails trying to be something or someone they're not. You be you. Seriously. Changing your personal character is a lot bigger than the scope of this book, but embracing who you are and how you act in certain situations can help you understand and embrace your brand character.

As we understand our brand character, we understand what we will and won't do on and off track. Then, we can build our best version of ourselves. It doesn't matter what it is. Go ahead and embrace your inner Dale Earnhardt, Jeff Gordon, Vaughn Gittin, Jr., or Jordan Taylor. You be you here. It's way easier to be true to yourself than to try to be true to something you're not. This isn't saying that you can't aspire to be like JR or Jordan Taylor, but it does mean that you should focus on racing your own way.

The I Will and I Won't list can also be stretchy. Think of them as promises to yourself that you really don't want to break. Breaks and mistakes will no doubt happen, but if you've been true to yourself and built these principles around your brand, those around you will say, "Wow, that was out of character. He or she must've been really upset." They'll assume an external factor must have prompted the deviation from your character.

In essence, brand character is how you will achieve your goals. We haven't even talked about those yet. The reason for that is the why and how are rooted deep in emotion and passion, and are the key to the way people around you react to you and your brand. After you've written out your I Will and I Won't list, reread it. What does it tell you about you? Can you boil it down to a sentence or better yet a phrase?

For me, it's: I'm passionate about winning and achieving my goals in a way I can be proud of.

THE MOST VISIBLE CARS IN THE FIELD

How does brand character for a team differ from that of an individual? Team character is built race after race and people watch a well-branded and consistent team. It starts with character—the how. So, what does brand character do for us as club racers? It serves as a guiding light, but it's more than that. Brand character is what sets the tone of your brand apart from the rest of the club racing brands out there.

When people evaluate racing teams to partner with or join, the character of that team, or who they are and how they are seen inside and outside of the paddock, is a big part of their decision.

The racing team's I Will and I Won't list will be quite different from the racer's one. This list will focus a lot more on the soul of the team and these will/won't phrases don't necessarily need to be in opposite pairs either.

Here are some examples:

- We will be resilient in the face of adversity
- We will be the most fun group in the paddock
- We will deliver the best-prepped cars to the track
- We will deliver outstanding support to our drivers
- We will not cut corners to save money
- We will not sacrifice safety for speed
- We will not be the first ones to turn out the lights
- We will have the most visible cars in the field
- We are the underdog, we are not the overdog

At first this is super difficult, especially if you set super-lofty goals in your I Will and I Won't list. Be realistic and know that it is difficult to get everybody rowing in the same direction at first, especially for a new team. Once the rules are set, it'll be easier to get processes and procedures in place to help guide the team. These should, for the most part, come pretty naturally.

For example, if you want part of your team's brand character to be delivering the best-prepped cars to the track, make sure you have or find the people who can do this. Develop the checklists to ensure that every time the cars go out on track, they are consistently well prepared. This also starts back at the shop with component replacement before failure and regular race car maintenance. Each component of a team's brand character builds on each other.

It's okay to strive for more here and set targets you want to achieve. Like your personal brand character, this needs to be true to you and not manufactured. It's here's who we are and here's who we want to be. These are great statements that will help guide you. As your team grows larger, you will likely find yourself reinforcing some of the this-is-how-we-do-this-around-here kinds of things.

These statements will help you in times of calm as well as in times of crisis. You find out so much more about yourself and your team when things are in crisis. You'll learn what is/is not statements you're willing to bend to get to the solution. For example, you may commit to having one of the most consistently, meticulously prepped cars in the paddock. Then in final practice, your driver hits the wall and you end up sending the car out with duct tape holding the hood down.

You do the best you can and prepare, but things happen and you know you'll likely be in this situation. So, to do your best to stay true to your brand character; you have tape the same color as the bodywork to blend it in. You drive the perception of prepared for anything and prepared for the racetrack the best you can. Eventually, it may mean you bring a back up car with you just in case.

Knowing your boundaries ahead of time will help you make decisions faster and more precisely during race weekends and beforehand. It's just one of many decisions you'll make for your team.

Brand character is all about being true to your vision and believing in your brand. Again, it's hard to talk about brand character without being preachy, but be true to yourself and your vision here and things will go much more smoothly for you when it's crunch time.

Your brand character will be a little like your soul and conscience. It's how you will be known to fans, competitors, series officials, friends, and family.

You've built a purpose and a character for your brand. We've talked a lot about the why and how of your club racing brand. Now we need to talk about what you're trying to do with this brand of yours and where you're going to take it. Brand goals are about where you are going and laying out the path to get there. Every brand has its own unique goals and we're going to build yours now. So, let's get to it!

4

BUILDING BRAND GOALS

It's 1994, and I just won the season championship and divisional runoffs.

We were at the awards banquet for the Land o' Lakes region of the Sports Car Club of America and I was nominated for both Driver of the Year and Rookie of the Year. A bunch of great drivers were nominated for both awards. I didn't think I had a shot at all.

I sat with my team, Mayhem Racing, in the ballroom at the Calhoun Beach Athletic Club. Rookie of the Year went to a phenomenal open wheel driver named Toby Cossette. They'd gotten to the end of the program and described each of us Driver of the Year nominees in turn, highlighting our performances and why we should be in the running for the award. Driver of the Year was about performance, personality, and involvement in the club.

Since I arrived in Minneapolis, I had been active in our local autocross club, the Minnesota Autosports Club (MAC). I attended monthly club meetings and eventually I was elected to the MAC board. Once I started road racing in 1993, I shifted my focus to the SCCA.

At Brainerd, my teammates, Mark Utecht and Wade Roggemann, and

I attended the worker meetings early in the morning to say thank you from Mayhem Racing. Before we headed to the worker meetings, we'd visit each corner station and drop off drinks or treats as a surprise for the workers. Our favorite surprise for them was bubbles—during our race's pace lap, the air was filled with bubbles and waving, smiling corner workers!

So, we were at the awards banquet, listening to the announcer speak about each nominee in turn. He got to the end of the list and shared my accomplishments from the 1994 season—CenDiv Champion, Land o' Lakes Champion, Divisional Runoffs Champion. Then, there was a pause, and he called out my name as the 1994 Land o' Lakes Driver of the Year.

I had assumed a more accomplished driver would win, not me—a young, rookie kid. I was completely unprepared to win the award. In a short but rambling acceptance speech I talked about how surprised I was and how proud I was of my team. I hadn't given a potential speech any thought and wasted a perfectly good platform to speak about my personal and brand goals. I wouldn't have called them that at the time, of course, but nevertheless, it was a wasted opportunity in front of a group of people willing to help.

I didn't have a plan for 1995. I didn't have a target or a goal for where I wanted to go other than the amorphous goal of becoming a professional driver. I was so busy putting one foot in front of the other that I hadn't thought about what should be next.

After the speech, two separate groups of people approached me to ask if I was interested in testing their car for the next season, 1995. I was super flattered and flustered. I didn't know exactly what they were offering and I wasn't comfortable pressing them on specifics. Somehow, I thought that I was supposed to know. I was embarrassed I didn't know and would have to ask, so I didn't. We sometimes make odd decisions in the moment.

Later, as I reflected, I wasn't sure if they had just asked me to pay to test their car, were offering a free ride, or what. As time went by, I eventually dismissed the conversations, assuming I misinterpreted their comments as offers. I didn't reach back out to either group—what was I thinking?!—and let the opportunities slip through my fingers.

Why did I respond that way? I think for two reasons, primarily. First, I hadn't thought out my next steps, my goals, or my career path. So, I had no idea how these offers would fit into my plan for my career.

Second, I held myself to an impossible standard and felt like I somehow should have known what they were talking about. Instead of asking a couple of clarifying questions, I nodded my head. I'm sure I came across as impossibly arrogant, but I just lacked the confidence to ask what I felt was an obviously dumb question. Everybody knew that I was new to the sport. They would have understood. It was me who did not.

It wasn't until many, many years later, after I'd grown up a little more, that I found out that both of the offers were serious and they were both looking for the next young, talented road racer to come test their car. They were lost opportunities for sure and one more reason to focus on goal setting for my brand.

This was an unfortunate mistake that I needed to make so I could learn from it. Once I realized what I had done, I committed myself to asking questions in the future and not worrying about seeming clueless.

BE SELFISH

Purpose, character, and goals help you point the arrow of your brand. You know your why and your how, but where are you pointing? Where are you going? A brand goal is more than what do you want to do when you grow up. It's why you race, how you race, and what you'll achieve. This one is a challenge, because we all have different reasons for racing.

What do you want your personal brand to be known for throughout the paddock and beyond? There is so much you can do to drive perception and visibility of your personal brand, but much of it starts with your brand goal. Let's work on that.

When you are developing your personal brand goals, I can't stress enough to take the time to really understand what you want your personal brand to be. It's much more than black hat vs. white hat. It's much more than how you interact with competitors and fans. This is where we as club racers can embrace our self-centeredness and focus on what we want to do and be. It's totally normal for this part to make you feel self-conscious.

When you put your personal branding goals on paper, being specific will guide you during the season and beyond. Your brand goal needs to be bigger than a goal for just one year. For your personal brand, you need a group of goals that build upon each other and point you towards an overarching goal.

As you build your brand goal, look back to your purpose and character. Are you building a brand goal that is consistent with your personal one—your You be You—and also setting a path towards something you strive for?

Some drivers are all focus and intensity on the track, but they are all about fun off track. Look at the personal brand that Jordan Taylor has built up around his character Rodney Sandstorm and all of the super-silly videos he puts out each week. The reason this works is that Jordan at his core is just flat-out goofy and he embraces it as a release from the serious business of driving the car.

Think about Vaughn Gittin, Jr. and his Ultimate Fun Haver brand that he has developed over several years. Vaughn competes hard and always has fun doing it. He is similar to Jordan in that his off-track exploits are where he lets loose. He always has a great time at every event he attends. It's him and it's part of his brand. His brand goal is to be the Ultimate Fun Haver.

There may be a day that Jordan or Vaughn aren't feeling it, but they show up with all their energy for their fans. It's a part of their brand and it's their job as the face of their personal brand to deliver.

CORPORATE BRAND GOALS

Here are some examples of corporate brand goal to help you get a handle on the types of things your club racing brand goals can point you towards.

- **LinkedIn:** Create economic opportunity for every member of the global workforce.
- **Southwest:** To be the world's most loved, most efficient, and most profitable airline.
- **Life is Good:** To spread the power of optimism.

- **TED:** To spread ideas.
- **Ganassi Racing:** To be the most professional and most admired team in motorsports.

I WANT TO ACHIEVE

Your brand goal is the third part of your why, how, and what trio.
Brand purpose is *the why*, the driving force of doing what you do.
Brand character is *the how*, is the soul and personality of your team brand.
Your brand goal is *the what*, the thing you want to accomplish as a team.

It's the thing you strive for, work long hours into the night for. The thing you strive to repeat every weekend. It's a deceptively simple question: What do you as a brand, or a team brand, want to achieve for yourself or deliver for others?

It can be a difficult one to develop because there are so many options. As Matt Martelli of Mad Media once told me, "Try, fail, and adjust. Just go, man!" Good words of advice for developing any set of brand goals.

So, who are you? What's your brand? Can you put it into words? How do you get there? What do you want to get out of your club racing? What do you want your personal brand to achieve?

They're all good questions, but how do we get to those truths?

Each step on our branding path is guided by the prior steps. Embrace your own selfishness here. Write it down. What is your goal for your personal racing brand? Do you want to be known as the best in your class, the most well-liked, the most fun? The theme here is to make the goal a big goal. An achievable goal, but a big goal. Your goal should be something you strive to achieve every time you step on track or connect with your followers.

The hardest thing here is to see that goal out there in the future. It's totally ok to write down one goal on the path and keep moving the goalposts as you achieve them. But, try this: focus on the biggest goal and let the steps in between fill themselves in as you and your brand grow.

You may be the driver who's always available to drive anything at the drop of a hat. Build your brand around that. Enhance it every time you communicate and make it your own. You may be the driver who's always willing to take chances on the path to victory—checkers or wreckers. Embrace it. Your goal is winning, damn the consequences.

The important thing here is to see where you want to go with your racing as a driver and as a brand. Do you want to be known as the nicest, the fittest, the best at what you do?

This goal setting for us as club racers goes across disciplines—drag racing, ice racing, rally, road racing, circle track, motocross, karting. It applies everywhere.

One thing you may notice is that I've left out things like turn professional and win races and championships. These are great goals to have. Absolutely! But they are personal goals, not personal brand goals. It's an important distinction. What you want to achieve personally and what you want your personal brand to achieve are separate, but dependent things. I've found the best way to separate them is to write them down.

I write "I want to achieve…" and "I want my brand to be known as…"

This process has helped me define my personal racing goals and my racing brand goals. They are two different things. My personal racing goals are very results oriented. I want to be the national champion in my class, the best amateur racer in the US in our class. My brand goals are to be well-respected, a fair but hard competitor, a smart marketer, and a racer who overachieves for his partners. I strive for success every time out but I do my best to stay consistent with my brand goals. I've definitely had brand failures from time to time when my temper and competitive spirit got the best of post-race me.

Those have been rare moments and we've all had them as racers. It's a passionate sport. My focus is not to let those slips define me and my brand. I focus on being true to myself and my brand as best as I can.

One thing, though: as you grow your brand, you evolve and your brand evolves. As you grow and expand in this sport, it is likely that you will change how you approach it. Brands are organic and grow and prosper with care and nurturing. Feed your brand, grow with it, and be true to yourself. Over the years, have you become more patient, more aggressive, more confident, funnier, more open, more closed?

Embrace change and mold your brand around you. Your personal brand is you after all. You will change and your brand should grow with you. This is the same for a team brand. As a team gains experience and confidence, tackles new challenges, grows, and becomes more professional, you may find some of the things you did when the brand was young no longer fit with the new image the brand is growing into.

On the flipside, you may find that some of the things you are doing now aren't in keeping with the spirit of the brand. You may need to re-evaluate and bend the brand back to your will a bit.

Brand goals also evolve and it's completely ok to start small and work your way past milestone after milestone. You may find your first brand goal was too easy to achieve and you're looking for the next step for your brand. That's totally okay. More than okay, it's great! You did it! Now, reach for the next one.

Here's a simple example of how to do this.

Let's for a moment assume that your brand goal is to be the most well-known, most visible driver in the club series you compete in. Go out and set yourself targets, measure your competition, deliver on those targets, and achieve your brand goal. Once you've achieved it, you need a next step. A natural one in this instance, is to move up a series or class and repeat your original brand goal of being the most well-known, most visible driver. Rinse and Repeat.

Each version of your brand goals starts small and builds upon success after success. Approaching brand goals this way can help you build momentum for your brand as you progress throughout your club racing career.

So, think hard about this. Write a lot of goals down for you, your personal brand, and your team brand. These three sets of goals (personal, personal brand and team brand) are intertwined but very separate. This part usually takes the longest as I find myself moving personal goals and brand goals from one column to another as I list them out. Use the sentence starters and build out four or five goals for you as a racer, you as your personal racing brand, and your team as its own racing brand.

ROWING IN THE SAME DIRECTION

Team branding is a little more complicated and it's a little trickier to get everybody pulling the oars in the same direction for the team. But, at the same time, a team vision is also a little easier to develop and execute. As we develop a set of team goals, we commit to them and the team members believe in and buy into the vision and the goal.

For a team, it could be service, expertise, preparation, experiences, fun, or any number of things. The goal is to have one goal. See what I did there? The team is headed in one direction—it could be with multiple cars and a ton of people—but it's via one dedicated mission. You want your team goals to become a shorthand for where your team brand is headed.

Your brand goal should be able to finish this sentence: We will…

The trick is to answer the question without saying, "…make money racing." Or, "…make my racing pay for itself." Or, "…win races and championships."

Those are outcomes, not brand goals. They're really good outcomes, but not brand goals. It's easy to end up with an outcome instead of a goal as they are so similar.

Here are some examples of club racing brand goals:

We will…

- be the most admired team in the paddock
- be the most fun team at each event
- be the team that helps everyone
- be the team everyone wants to drive for

Brand goals build upon brand purpose and character. As my team developed a plan to go into endurance sports car racing, we felt we needed to do it with a new brand instead of with Fritz Wilke Racing, because the brand goals were so different.

Our new brand, Flying Ghost Racing Team (FGRT), has a purpose and soul of its own. Let's take a quick look at FGRT's brand goals and see how we got to where we are. It starts with the brand purpose as we've discussed earlier, but it flows into brand character and finally into the brand goal.

WHY DO WE DO THIS SPORT?
(BRAND PURPOSE)

- **Version 1:** We believe unforgettable experiences changes people's lives.
- **Version 2:** We believe racing creates unforgettable experiences.
- **Version 3:** We love making racing memories.
- **Final:** We create great racing memories!

HOW DO WE DO IT?
(BRAND CHARACTER)

- **Version 1:** We deliver unforgettable experiences and change lives by fulfilling racing dreams in meticulously prepared racing cars at tracks across North America.

- **Version 2:** We create unforgettable experiences in our race cars at tracks across North America.
- **Version 3:** We put you in our race cars!
- **Final:** We are a fun and competitive arrive and drive team. We prep the cars, you have the fun!

WHAT DO WE DO?
(BRAND GOALS)

- **Version 1:** We rent seats in our race cars at North America's greatest racetracks. Wanna race?
- **Version 2:** We rent race seats in our race cars.
- **Version 3:** We can put you in our race cars. We're renting out seats in our cars now! Wanna race?
- **Final:** We help our drivers make amazing memories!

As you think about your team brand goals, you'll go through several versions. Keep on working at it until you cut out all the business-book language (look at that first one in brand character. Ugh!) and really get at the why, how, and what of what your brand does and intends to keep on doing. Even now, those above will evolve and grow as FGRT grows as a team.

If you're still having trouble, it can sometimes help to put the phrase, "Our goal is to…" at the front of the goals part. It reminds you what direction you're heading in.

Let's look a little more closely at the FGRT goal, "We help racers make amazing memories." It's focused on experiences and memories.

Our team goal is to help the renters have amazing memories that they'll take home with them. How do we ensure their experiences are amazing? This will be our guiding light. This goal helps us set up our team strategy from first contact through the last handshake goodbye at the end of the weekend.

It is this trio of elements of a brand—brand goals, brand character, and brand purpose—that helps guide our brand journey. Every great brand started somewhere and often those brand goals and brand purposes morphed over the years as the world changed, but the character and soul of the great brands generally stay the same.

Apple nailed their brand character during their Think Different campaign. They said that they don't think the same as other companies, that they value design and ease of use over pure performance. Their company builds products to make the world a better place. It has been core to that company for decades.

Lots of what your team will do and how you will present yourself as a team will be driven by your purpose, character, and goals. These will help guide you as you reach out to partners, select drivers, hire technicians and engineers, and engage friends and family. Even something like brand colors can be influenced by your brand goals. You'll find yourself repeating, "Remember, we're XYZ," when evaluating an idea or designing the next bit of kit for the team.

If you're the team leader, take some time to think about the image you project to the world. If you're a team member, think about how you live up to the team brand goals on track and off. If you're a driver, how do you fit? Does your personality mesh with, contrast, or complement the team brand? All of these will help you as you do the work to define your team brand.

Once the team has fully bought in to the idea of what the team brand stands for, things come easier because everybody knows how their actions fit within the goals. If the goal is a championship and the car is broken within the first hour, the team will work like mad to get it back out because every point matters. If the team goal is fun, then they will spend more time on hospitality and the paddock area than others might. If the team goal is service, then the customer will always be right…as long as they can afford it.

Your brand goal, what you want your brand to stand for and what you want your brand to be, will continue to guide you throughout the branding process. Once you've completed this step of defining your brand goals for you and your team, we need to move on to finding, refining, and developing your unique brand voice.

5

FINDING YOUR BRAND VOICE

It's 2009. I'm a newly appointed Mustang brand manager and I'm standing at the lectern at the Mid-American Shelby Meet in Tulsa, Oklahoma.

My heart pounded in my ears as I looked out at a crowd of friends and Shelby Mustang enthusiasts, preparing to give my very first end-of-event keynote speech.

I worked on the speech for hours, but it still felt unfinished. My favorite boss ever, Robert Parker, had assured me it would be the easiest speech I'd ever given. In the end, like with most things, he was so right.

I've had a love-hate relationship with public speaking. I love it when I'm doing it, but hate the thought of it and often put off prepping for it.

My speech started with a series of video clips of the new 2010 Mustang in camouflage. It was a tease for our enthusiasts. I set the intro of the video to the start of the Van Halen song *Everybody Wants Some*. Rhythmic drums supported Eddie Van Halen's haunting guitar chords.

I stood there, at the lectern, waiting for the first image to come up on the black screen. I had forgotten how long the start of the music was before the first guitar chord. There I stood, for a full 45 seconds of black screen with drums and guitar playing over the loudspeakers.

About 25 seconds in, people started whispering to each other—does he know there's nothing on the screen, what should we do? People get *really* uncomfortable when someone is up on stage, not saying anything. In an inspired moment, I leaned in to the mike with a smartass smile on my face and in a muted voice said, "Wait for it...."

Just at that moment, the first chord popped and an image flashed on the screen of the new Mustang in camo. With each new chord came another flash of a camouflaged image of the yet-to-be-released Mustang with Eddie Van Halen rocking out over the PA!

I've got *Everybody Wants Some* playing in the background as I write this and I'm smiling with the memories of that night.

It was a great start to one of my favorite public speeches of all time. I built the presentation around our new marketing theme of embracing our enthusiasts, who we called Mustang Nation. It was a newish idea in 2009 and we were running with it.

The presentation featured images of all the influential leaders of the Shelby club—including Carroll, of course, and leaders of the Mustang world in general. I had taken pictures of all the leaders of our Mustang Nation during the three-day event and these images played on the screen as I described how important our enthusiasts were to the brand.

It was my first time speaking as a representative of a truly great brand and I felt the pressure of all the great brand managers watching me to make sure I nailed the tone. That's why it took me such a long time to write the speech. It was a combination of stage fright and a determination to get it just right.

The Mustang brand is about freedom and fun, confidence, and power and performance, without the bad-ass, bad-boy branding that Camaro focuses on. Shelby Mustang owners are a slightly different breed of Mustang owners—they embody all the core mustang traits and add a dash of exclusivity and insider knowledge.

My role as a Mustang brand manager was to launch the Mustang and beat Camaro first and foremost. But it was also to embrace our faithful and enlist them in the mission to sell more Ford vehicles.

That weekend, I had learned the true responsibility of being the leader of the brand. I wasn't the face of the brand, but I was the Mustang rep on the ground and I had a responsibility to live up to for Mustang.

As you may know by now, racing and performance are my passion and this was an easy jacket to slip into while working as Mustang brand manager. I could be true to myself and tweak it for the Mustang on-stage moments. At first, I felt very self-conscious as we all do when we step on stage to represent our companies or families. Once I embraced the similarities and differences of my personality vs. that of the Mustang brand manager, things came easier.

My personal brand became intermixed with that of the Mustang brand and I am glad to have had an impact on the Mustang brand in my own way. As I look back at my career at Ford, my time as Mustang brand manager and a performance and enthusiast manager remains my favorite part of my career at Ford. In many ways, it was this experience that helped me define my own personal brand voice. I used my love of history and passion for motorsports to grow the Mustang brand into the 2010s and beyond.

HOW DO YOU SPEAK?

How are the pro drivers you follow or cheer for different from each other? What do their personal brands stand for? Are they the super-aggressive hard charger? Or are they the mellow, silent, but deadly type? What about funny, silly, or goofy? And are they the same personality on track and off?

Voice is a tricky thing to manage. Think of someone trying to do your social media for you. How do you communicate the tone you shoot for? How do you help them understand how you say things?

You've built your brand purpose, your brand character, and your brand goals. Your brand voice is another trip into the how. Your brand voice is how you communicate to the world. Use your own voice and your team's voice when talking to the world as a race car driver or team owner. Your personality needs to come through. If you're a smartass, then be a smartass. If you have a dry sense of humor, then embrace it. If you're silly, be silly. People who know you will know it's you. People who are meeting you for the first time will get to know the right version.

It's easy to think of your brand voice and your brand personality as interchangeable. They are very similar and interrelated, but your brand voice refers to the words and tone you use, while your brand personality is the way your brand acts and reacts to the world on and off track.

Building your brand voice starts by going back to your core, the elements of branding we've already covered: brand purpose, brand goals, and brand character.

Here are a few tricks to help you discover and strengthen your racing brand voice. Think about a few adjectives that describe you—how would your racing friends describe you? Think about the language you use to describe your experiences and the world around you. This is the ultimate You be You here. You may want to soften a few of the sharp edges or embrace them—it's up to you. Be true to yourself.

A STOMPING NEW BRAND

It can help to think of your voice as a mashup. A good approximation of my brand voice is a mashup of several easy-to-imagine qualities: quirky British-style humor; a drive to make the best of any situation; thankful humility; a good brag when I'm excited; polished grammar and spelling; a broad experience base; and a thorough understanding of racing history.

One of my favorite examples of using a mashup to communicate a complex concept came from Jim Farley, now CEO of Ford. When Jim started as head of marketing at Ford, he tasked a group of us to figure out what to do with the Mercury brand. Our options were limited: kill it or reinvent it. Both had similar price tags and Jim wanted to see options.

Jim is a leader who asks questions to learn. This was completely alien to the Ford Way. The Ford Way response to a question from an executive was to salute, go study the problem, and report back quickly. At the time, the assumption was that a Ford exec didn't want an answer right there in the meeting. If they asked a question, they were really giving you an assignment—go figure it out, now!

Jim wasn't brought up with the Ford Way. He was cerebral and had vast experience launching the Scion brand and also as the head of Lexus. Jim was, and continues to be, an unusual leader of intelligence and vision. He was often many steps ahead of the questions he was asking and he wanted to bring people along on the journey to help them understand where his head was, where he was going, and where he wanted them to go next.

However, when Jim first came to Ford, he'd say something along the lines of, "Have you thought about X?" and the immediate response would be, "Yes, sir, we'll get right back to you on that!" At first, Jim was super patient as he tried to work his magic through the Ford system. However, several times his frustration shone through as he made it very clear that he wanted an actual answer to the question he had asked. Yes or no would do just fine.

The reason for his building fury was he simply wanted a clear understanding of where we, Ford marketing, were in the process. He wanted to guide us towards the portion of the industry he wanted us to explore. Those upfront questions were his way of finding where we were on his mental map. Us, saluting and diving into each yes/no question as if each question was a request for a research project, was a colossal waste of time.

Many times, Jim was so far out in front of the subject that he just needed us to come along on the journey with him. He'd pretty much seen it all and wanted us to understand his perspective. It was painful for me to see the Ford Way reaction of our leaders to Jim's questions. In Jim's mind, I suspect, a leader asks questions of his team and does not expect them to blindly follow direction.

Back to Mercury. I was new to Ford at this point and I was pretty sure that I could see what he was doing, trying to get everybody to come along with him on the journey. My dad was CEO of our family business and I had seen him use a very similar technique of asking questions to get his team to follow and understand his vision.

Jim's frustrations and fury at the idiocy of the Ford Way of taking every question as an executive assignment soon became legendary. Ironically, it was exactly those who couldn't imagine that he actually wanted an answer to a question who experienced his wrath the most.

During the project to save Mercury, we saw this many times. We brought lots of proposals to him—everything from an all-hybrid brand, an all-green brand with a portion of the profits going to green initiatives, an ultra-luxury brand above Aston Martin, and even a hot rod, all-performance brand. Guess who that last one came from....

Jim looked at us one day with real pain in his eyes and asked us something along the lines of, "Please listen. I want to see a mashup of the following brands: Saturn, Mini, Harley-Davidson, Scion, and Pontiac."

The people in the room nodded and said something like, "Yes, sir. Okay, got it," and left without asking a single clarifying question. They were on their way to deliver on an executive assignment to go build that brand.

As I was new at the time, building the framework of this fell to me. Pretty quickly, I learned no one had any idea what Jim was actually asking us. Each person in that room understood each of those brands a little differently. Jim had asked us to mash up the brands, but we didn't understand which parts of those brands he wanted mashed. It was quickly becoming a mess.

I realized that, as the most junior person in the room, and the most inexperienced marketer, I could probably reach out directly to Jim, then head of Ford marketing, to find out what he wanted us to do. I could ask him what aspects of those five brands he wanted us to blend.

I got the okay from my boss and reached out to Jim. Jim replied right away with a note that started off apologizing for going too fast and laid out exactly what he wanted to see. He said something like, "Take the no haggling from Saturn, the badassery from Harley, the customization from Mini, the bravery of Scion, and the performance of Pontiac and you'd have a stomping new American youth brand in Mercury."

I put that together for my boss and the concept gained traction. We all got super-excited about this new, reimagined, and much more awesome Mercury. We even had concept car artwork created that hangs on the walls at Ford's Product Development Center to this day. Unfortunately, in the short term, it was easier and more cost effective to cut the Mercury brand than to reinvest in and re-imagine it. This was during the same period that we were working to shed all the non-Ford and non-Lincoln brands.

This remains an example I use when trying to explain voice and the pitfall we all experience when we try to illustrate an example. It's important when explaining voice to others that you provide multiple examples and specifics.

We often communicated visually at Ford and I found that I needed at least three images to convey any idea visually. If we were trying to say purple, then each one of the images better be purple or people were going to go off on a tangent of something else that spoke to them individually in those images.

For instance, if I ask you to describe an architect, you may say an artist or a visionary, but I may be thinking about architects as independent businesspeople or entrepreneurs or something else completely. We can't assume that everyone gets us or understands our thought process. However, if you put the architect with a lawyer and a doctor, you'd see professionals. If you put the architect with a business owner and a leader, you'd see entrepreneurs. If you put the architect with a painter and sculptor, you'd see artists. It's about managing the context.

It's the same when helping others understand your voice. Your brand's voice is your way of controlling context. This will become especially important when we get to the chapters on social media.

So, what does managing voice do for us? It puts a personality behind the brand. The words are important, especially so when you communicate via text on social media. Tone is everything and if there is one thing you take away from this chapter on voice, it is this: understand and embrace the tone of your brand voice.

Your voice, your tone, is your unique perspective on the world. It is your job to let your voice shine through all of your communications. It doesn't matter whether it's via press release, via actual speech or interviews, or via text on social media or online forums. Embrace your brand voice and be yourself. Enhance the parts of your voice that you enjoy and downplay the parts of your voice that you don't.

GET OUT OF JAIL FREE CARD

Be aware of the consequences of your actions and your words. Many partners are leery of teaming up with brands that they see as loose cannons or politically outspoken. This is a fine line to walk with your voice. It's important that you are authentic to your core brand values and purpose, and don't be afraid of being you. Be outraged when appropriate, be passionate when appropriate, be in awe or as thoughtful as it makes sense for your brand. Your brand voice should not be a just-the-facts, ma'am, type of experience for your audience.

On the flipside, many partners will have a get out of jail free card written into their contracts. If you do something, say something, post something that is offensive to them or against their corporate values, they can drop you. These caveats have been written into most of my contracts in racing. Corporate brands do not want to be forced to stay connected with a racing brand or personality that goes off the rails and embarrasses them. These limitations have the potential to turn your personal voice towards the bland side.

Don't lose yourself in your quest to please everyone with a middle-of-the-road brand voice. Here's where You be You comes into play. Just be yourself. Draw the partners you want towards you. Understand that you need to be a little more circumspect, but be the best version of yourself. People connect with and admire personality. Often our brand voice will come out in interviews or on social media. Embrace your uniqueness there. Nobody remembers bland interviews.

At first, I found that this was one of the hardest lines to walk, but one of my partners, seeing me embracing blandness, told me that they signed me because of me and my personality and not this bland version. Be yourself, don't embarrass your partners, and make them proud of their association with you and your brand.

If you're outspoken and your brand is outspoken, be yourself. Speak your mind. Embrace your personality and lean into it.

There's one arena, however, where you should do your best to control your emotions and that's when you're on the wrong end of a collision or on-track event. Always try to give the other driver the benefit of the doubt, even if it is ridiculously obvious. You can be upset, angry even, if that's in character for your brand, but no one cheers for the complaining racer for very long. That act loses its novelty quickly.

You can say you're going to go find out what the hell happened, but keep the direct blame out of the equation. The "everyone else on track is an idiot" schtick is pretty lame. We've all seen it and it gets old fast. Be careful of slipping into this, especially when you're very angry and a mic is put in your face to get just this reaction.

Do your best to disconnect the accident from the person who caused it. We're racers and we all take responsibility for our actions. It's likely the person at fault will do just that. It doesn't benefit you to judge first in this instance, and certainly not when you come across as "everyone else but me is an idiot." That is not the way to win followers.

On a positive note, though, be excited when you win and do it in your brand voice. Your tone, your excitement, your passion comes through your brand voice. Choose your tone and enhance it with each interaction.

One of the trickier things to manage is your voice on social media, as we rarely type as we speak. Take your time when you post to manage your voice and soon it will become natural to slip into that branded voice when you post for your club racing brand, personal or team.

Look at brands or athletes you admire and see how consistent they are or not with their brand voice. Notice how jarring it is when a brand speaks out of voice. Typically, this is when someone at corporate has a specific message they want to promote and they only see the platform as a loudspeaker rather than as a branded voice. Sometimes these instances can be so out of voice that you stop and wonder for a moment if the account got hacked.

Ironically, if the person or people that wanted to communicate with the loudspeaker spent a little time bending the promotion, statement, or whatever to the brand voice, they'd be better off all around. Making a silly brand tackle serious issues more often than not ends in a hollow statement. Letting that silly brand tackle the serious issue in its own irreverently direct way will go much further and have much more resonance when it is said with the power of the true brand voice behind it.

This is a hard one to master and I've found that the best way to master my brand voice is to be true to myself and speak with people and online as I speak with friends and family—just being myself.

WE DON'T DO FEAR

Here are a few notable examples of brands with a well-known voice or style of communicating.

Wendy's brand voice has taken on a slightly snarky, but fearless voice when it comes to promoting their product differences vs. their direct competition. The thing that makes the Wendy's brand voice so powerful is that it stays so consistent that it's almost a brand as a person.

Another brand voice that has become almost the embodiment of a person is Duluth Trading Company's voiceover and lumberjack guy in their ads. Duluth Trading is all about apparel for the jobsite. They talk as if they've just come from the jobsite and focus on the things that matter to them—toughness, quality, and shirts that stay tucked in. They do it in a voice that makes you think of the team at Duluth Trading Company as a person and that person's voice is the brand voice.

Harley Davidson's brand voice is personified by their bold, aggressive, and confident approach to life. Their Screw it, Let's Ride campaign from the 2008 financial crisis was the perfect Harley Davidson-voiced approach to the financial uncertainty of that time.

The text of the print ad is here:

> WE DON'T DO FEAR. Over the past 105 years in the saddle, we've seen wars, conflicts, depression, recession, resistance, and revolutions. We've watched a thousand hand-wringing pundits disappear in our rear-view mirror. But every time, this country has come out stronger than before. Because chrome and asphalt put distance between you and whatever the world can throw at you. Freedom and wind outlast hard times. And the rumble of an engine drowns out all the spin on the evening news. If 105 years have proved one thing, it's that fear sucks and it doesn't last long. So screw it, let's ride.

The tone of the ad was perfect. Harley signaled their bold approach to life, the positivity and confidence of Harley owners, and their we-got-this approach to life. It's about leaving your cares behind and enjoying your time, clearing the mechanism of the doubters and negativity, and focusing on the now.

Brand voice is all about being true to yourself, your purpose, your character, and your goals. Sometimes, like Harley, it's about being true to yourself even if not everybody likes it. Whatever, says Harley, we don't live to make you happy. If you don't like it, go do something else. We'll be just fine enjoying ourselves over here.

GRAB THE MIC

As we work to develop our brand voice, we will infuse the brand elements we've built so far with a voice and a life of their own. As club racers, our brand voice is how we interact with others. It is our megaphone and microphone for conversations with partners, potential partners, and competitors. Your club racing brand voice sets you apart from your competitors. Embrace your own personal tone and amplify it. Talk about the things that make you wonder, make you laugh, and make you cringe. Put the soul into your brand through your brand communication.

With a team brand, always speak as a "we" or as "our team." The more you stay consistent with your team brand voice, the more memorable it will become. You can define this voice as professional, serious, curious, interesting, unusual, quirky, or whatever. When you define it, you emphasize the soul and person behind the brand in each interaction you and your team have.

Brand voice and brand personality are intertwined and are hard to separate. In the next chapter, we'll focus on how brand personality can enhance and amplify our brand voice.

6

YOUR BRAND PERSONALITY

It's February 1995. I'm finishing the build of my new road racing ITA CRX and starting my very first season of ice racing with Mayhem Racing.

I sought out a group of local ice racers in Minneapolis to get started. While asking questions about ice racing, the conversation turned to my ITA CRX. I had sold my 1993 car to buy the ITC Civic. Then, I sold that to buy the ITA CRX. My plan was to sell the CRX at the end of 1995 to pay for my first pro car. World Challenge was where I wanted to compete next.

I didn't know that most new professionals didn't own their race cars like we club racers do. In 1994, I competed in 16 races and spent nearly as much as I would have done to rent a season in a World Challenge car.

Later that afternoon, while talking with the ice racers in Minneapolis, I explained my goal to race in World Challenge the following year once the ITA car was sold. From time to time, I ask the wrong questions or catch the right people at the wrong moment. This was one of those times.

The response to my dream of pro racing from an ice racer I admired was,

"How old are you? All the pros have been racing since they turned seven. You're 15 years late to the party. You don't have a chance at your age."

I was 25.

Today, I would dismiss that response and chalk it up to someone having a bad day. But I was new and super impressionable. I took this as gospel. I put my dreams of going pro on the shelf because it seemed, without my realizing it, the pro door was already closed to me by that time. I was 25 and washed up. Man, if I could go back and talk to my younger self that day....

Earlier in 1995, I had reached out to Honda. I still don't know how I got the number for Charlie Cornutt at Honda Performance in California. I asked for setup advice on the CRX. It never occurred to me to ask questions about running in a pro series. He gave me Parker Johnstone's Firehawk CRX setup and cautioned me that Parker liked his cars loose. A little loose indeed!

I entered a race with the ITA CRX at Road America. It was the last time I'd race at Road America until 2017. We'd won at Brainerd and finished second to another Honda. We headed to Road America for the SCCA divisional race there.

On the fourth lap of qualifying, I entered turn one in the draft behind a friend. Once I committed to throttle, I needed to stay on it to keep the rear end in line. If I lifted at all, the rear would step out and the car would come around.

As we entered one, I saw the front tires of my friend's car turn into the corner more than the corner required. He was pushing and slowing up, coming back to me. We weren't far apart. I could hit him in the middle of the corner and send him off into the outside wall or try to back up from him.

I curled my toes and my car immediately jumped sideways, the rear tires sliding over the exit curb. I caught it once. Then it hooked and slid towards the inside wall. It was the only time I was truly scared in a race car.

The concrete wall—right near the old Chicago Tribune bench—was taller than the car. There were no tires there and I was sliding towards it driver's side first. I tried to get small and into the center of the car. I knew hitting my head on the wall at this speed would be really, really bad.

At the last moment, I let go of the wheel and grabbed my belts. I hit on the left front and crushed the car flat from the hood emblem to the A-Pillar; it rotated and crushed the rear from the B-Pillar to the rear center emblem. My head went through the window net and bent the rod 90 degrees. This was long before HANS devices. The first impact pushed the car away from the wall and rotated just enough that I escaped hitting my head on the wall.

There are tires along that stretch of wall now. Behind the tires, my yellow and blue paint is still there, all these years later.

The car was a banana-shaped disaster. The undamaged passenger side door was wrinkled like covers kicked to the end of the bed. My crew chief, Joe Huttle, and I had built this car in a little detached garage behind my apartment and now, it was destroyed. My competitors came by to check on me and eventually buy the salvageable parts off the wreck.

My plans of racing, winning, and selling the car came apart. It took me a long time to get past that wreck at Road America, mentally and financially. But, from the ashes of that 1995 season came an entry into the car business and, later, business school and a career change into corporate marketing.

Ultimately, this event would inspire me to get back into racing in a completely new way. The lessons we need to learn sometimes arrive on our doorstep in the strangest of ways.

VOLCANOES, TANKS AND FREEDOM!

So, what is the personality of your brand? You differentiate yourself and your brand in how you react to praise and criticism, success and failure. Are you funny, serious, or determined? No matter what the soul of your brand is, be true to your own personality.

Your personal brand personality is pretty straightforward—it is you being you. It is you speaking in your own voice, you defining your character, you being true to the best and most frustrating versions of yourself.

A great example of a brand with character and soul is Old Spice. Check out this silly Twitter exchange between them and Taco Bell from summer 2012:

> @oldspice: Why is it that "fire sauce" isn't made with any real fire? Seems like false advertising.
>
> @tacobell: @oldspice Is your deodorant made with really old spices?
>
> @oldspice: @tacobell Depends. Do you consider volcanos, tanks and freedom to be spices?

And this one:

> @oldspice: When opportunity knocks, punch a hole in the door and shake its hand like a man.

This is a brand true to its soul and its over-the-top mockery of its own personality. Old Spice stays on brand and on brand personality super well.

Think of some other brands that stay true to their soul and their unique personality. Consider how they handle criticism, success, and failure.

We all know that racing comes with risks and ups and downs. At the end of each event, there is only one winner. How do you deal with the inevitable accident? How do you handle success and how do you manage conflicts?

Thinking about each of these questions ahead of time will help you manage these situations when you are on stage and in the public eye. Your approach will speak loudly about your brand. It's not only in the public eye that you display your brand personality, but also in the quiet of your thoughts. How does your brand deal with these ups and downs? How does your brand react?

Let's put together some strategies. Take a look back at the brand you have crafted and let's put a soul into it. Let's put a real person, or people, behind your personal and team brand. The rest of this chapter is going to boil down to one phrase: be real.

That's it. Put your own spin on events on the track and off, absolutely, but people love people, not automatons. People follow people, not computer-generated content.

For many who follow us racers, they are seeking to see the world through our eyes—all of it, the adventure, the speed, the thrill, the competition, the highs and lows, the wrecks, the car failures, the wins, and the losses. All of it. Really. All of it. It's okay to have a crap day.

You and your brand personality are going to experience all of these emotions. How you and your brand deal with these is completely under your control.

YOU'RE THE DRIVER, WHAT ARE *YOU* GOING TO DO ABOUT IT?

Let's start with one of my favorite job interview questions of all time: "How do you deliver bad news?"

Shit happens on track—cars crash, you run off track, you hit stuff, you hit each other, cars break, slow cars hold you up, cars race out of class, it rains, and cars take your line. So, how does your brand deliver bad news?

For each of us, our answer is going to be slightly different. Your sport, karting, drag racing, circle track, dirt, road racing, powerboating, or motocross is going to be a big part of the equation. Look around: How do others in your sport deal with adversity? Are there brands or personalities that you admire or make you cringe for how they overcome problems on track?

Here are some strategies I use for dealing with and delivering bad news.

I do my best to think before I speak. I really do try. My partners don't want to support that not-my-fault kind of personality. I'm not a total turn-the-other-cheek kind of guy either. I do get frustrated when stupid crap happens out on track. Behind the scenes I am furious and get it out of my system, but on the mic, I try to understand and forgive.

Most of the time it's just a mistake, not intentional. We are all working our way up the ladder of the club ranks and we all are going to make mistakes. How we deal with it sets us apart from the rest. I focus on giving them the benefit of the doubt, just as I would expect if the roles were reversed.

How do I deal with a mistake when I am clearly at fault? The first thing I do when we finish the session is go check on the person I made contact with and make sure they are ok. I wait a little bit for us all to get settled, though. It lets them vent at me, and, since it's my fault, I probably deserve it. I've had reactions from my competitors that range from understanding to…not. This won't work for everyone; it's just how I deal with my mistakes.

Another situation that comes up is dealing with a mistake by my team that costs performance on track. I'm in their hands and their machinery is in my hands. It is truly a team sport. I've had loose wheels, hub failures, radio failures, dead batteries, and lots of other unique failures over the years. Each of those failures was the sum of a bunch of mistakes.

The most frustrating situation I had was when we accidentally swapped tire pressures front to rear on the race car at Grattan Raceway. I went from having a quick but loose race car to one that was impossibly tight. I was swearing loudly on the radio, bitching and moaning lap after lap. All of my energy was focused on the problem.

The calm voice of my race engineer, Craig Capaldi, came over the radio. "Okay, the car sucks to drive. You're the driver, what are *you* going to do about it?" Craig is a super-talented ex-pro driver and drove my car for several years in World Challenge before I bought it. He also has stood on the podium in Trans-Am. He knows his stuff. He also knows how to wind me up.

At this point none of us knew what was going on. I took my finger off the radio button and got all the rest of the swearing out of my system and made up some creative new titles for Craig! After I calmed down a bit, I described in detail what was happening and asked how I could drive around it. He told me. Then, I put my head down and drove.

That simple comment from Craig turned my focus back to where it should have been. It was a "show me what you've got" moment. Every time since then, when I'm in a car that goes from awesome to diabolical, I remember that comment. I'm sure he said it with a watch-this smile on his face: "What are *you* going to do about it?"

When I finished the race and was asked how it went, I was already thinking of it as a handling issue. Later in the debrief behind closed doors, we figured out what happened. To this day, I ask about pressures and if the lug nuts have been torqued before I go out for each session. It's become a little like my touchstone.

We will all have moments when our passions get the best of us. Racing is, after all, a sport built on passion. There's a reason we love it and tie so much of our emotion to our motorsports experience. It's completely okay to say, "Don't talk to me right now," or "I need a little space" when you get out of the car.

EMBRACE GRACE

You see it a lot in this sport—the car was awesome, my competition was great, I'm just lucky to have brought home the win, blah blah blah…. How do you and your brand make a victory lane speech memorable?

When you win, do your best to embrace grace. Yeah, you finished up a lap on everyone else, but focus on the car and the team. Yeah, you made an amazing pass on the last lap, but focus on how you set it up and how you delivered. Focus on you and not on your competitor. With this exception, be true to your brand. If you're a white hat brand, then praise your competitors. If you're a black hat brand, then it's totally okay to say things like, "I knew I had them covered."

One thing I've found that works during the podium interviews is to find someone nearby to compliment, whether it's my competitors sharing the podium or a partner in the audience. I thank them for a great race, a great product, for pushing me in the race—something like that.

Each of our personalities are different, so take these stories and ideas as an inspiration and not direction. You do you.

More than anything, as you think about your brand's personality, understand how important emotional intelligence is to us as racers. Brands under stress either perform or they don't. Think of your brand's emotional intelligence as being a bit of your racing resilience. Find a way to keep your chin up and put a positive spin on things, no matter how wrong they seem at the time.

Sometimes, luck isn't with us and it is then that we find out who we really are as racers and what our brand personality and character is to become.

ON STAGE

I was lucky to spend time with celebrities, broadcasters, and racing drivers during my career at Ford. Each one was on stage during their time with me and each had a different take on how they should interact with the Mustang or Ford guy. But you know what: each stayed true to their on-stage brand personality.

Drivers were all over the place, fun, crazy, quiet, each has a spot in my memory. Broadcasters tended to be a little more serious, but ready with a quick laugh and a smile. That's what we're trying to go for with your brand personality. Emphasize the portions of your personality that you can be true to and above all be yourself.

Some of my favorite interactions were in real-world situations. Like, running into Rick DeBruhl, who I'd worked with at Barrett-Jackson, at the gas station outside of the Indianapolis Motor Speedway on his way to the track. Or chatting with Tommy Kendall at the airport while waiting to board a plane. Sitting in the hauler with Vaughn Gittin Jr. at GRIDLIFE discussing marketing strategies. Coffee with Tanner Foust while sitting out a flight delay in

Detroit. Chatting with Gary Bennett while he cleaned up at a blackjack table in Las Vegas.

We rarely get to see the everyday personality of celebs like these as they are *on* so much of the time. For many of them, they are who you see on TV in real life. Like all of us, they have on times and off times.

For us as club racers, our branded personality will be very close to our real personality. Maybe we're a bit more us than others in the spotlight, but we're really close to who we are as a brand. Whatever your personality, stay true to it for your personal brand. It's what got you to where you are.

EXTEND THE REACH OF YOUR BRAND

We're building the soul of your brand and developing an understanding of the components of that soul as we work our way through this book. We've already focused on how to stay true to the foundations of your brand: purpose, character, goals, voice, and personality.

Again, your brand personality is mostly you being you, just a bit extra. It's your best foot forward that you choose to emphasize. You decide how you enable and expand your brand personality.

The strategies we've discussed in this chapter are intended to help you think through situations that you will likely find yourself in, by your own creation or not. Each interaction is an opportunity to support and grow your brand.

Know when you are on stage and when you are not. While You be You always applies to your personal brand, it's alright to be a little more you when you know you're on stage. You are the brand owner and you are guiding the ship here. To paraphrase my engineer, "You are the driver of your brand. What are *you* going to do about it?"

One key way our brand personality helps us as club racers is that it helps bring your passion to the forefront. It is this curation of brand personality—You be You, right, but a little more—that elevates the exposure and reach of your brand beyond club racing and into other areas.

As you develop and enhance your brand personality and voice, you will continue to breathe soul into your club racing brand. Your club racing brand will quickly take on a life of its own and people will talk about your club team brand as if it is a person instead of a group of people pulling the oars in one direction.

How do we keep your brand on the right path given all the chaos that surrounds us every race week? We build and protect your brand through a strong focus on consistency. Consistency is key to a brand's ability to act as a shorthand and it builds upon a strong brand foundation. If the foundation is strong, it is easier to correct when things stray from the mission.

Let's figure out how to create a consistent presence for your brand!

7

BUILDING BRAND CONSISTENCY

It's Fall of 1992. I bought my first race car with money my grandmother left me when she passed.

Over the winter of 1992-93, we built that car, a 1984 Honda CRX, into a race car in Mark's garage with a bolt-in rollcage. I was on the stringiest of shoestring budgets. I bought all my safety equipment used except my shoes. The only new thing on the car was the rollcage.

I couldn't afford to paint the exterior, so I left it stock blue and gray. I put large vinyl numbers and the team name on the side of my car in the team font. The only difference from the team theme was that my numbers were white so we could see them better on the blue background.

I kept the CRX licensed for the street. I drove it to the track in 1993 instead of trailering it as I had no budget for a tow vehicle. It was pretty funny to see all the looks I got in my stickered-up car driving down the highway.

At that time, Mayhem Racing was one of the few multicar club racing teams with cars in similar liveries. This is far more common now in club racing, but it was rare in the early 90s. Each of us won often, which was another element of our continued presence at the track. We were now four: Mark, Tom, me, and a new addition to the team, Wade Roggemann.

When Wade joined the team in the Spring of 1993, he had an RX-7 that was painted in a cool scheme of white with a blue slash. It had bright yellow numbers with a pink shadow behind them. The numbers and letters were in the Mayhem Racing team font. It looked like a Mayhem car.

In fall of 1993, I sold the CRX. I used the money to purchase an already-built 1985 Honda Civic race car for the 1994 season. It was white with a red checkerboard livery. I added the Mayhem Racing logo and black, team-styled numbers on the side.

Mark was taking a year off racing and he offered to be my crew chief for 1994. He would tow my car to the races, prepare it, and keep it running. We brought the car to Blackhawk Farms in Rockton, Illinois in early April for the first race of the 1994 season.

I qualified the car on pole for my class and I was leading my first SCCA race! With just a few laps to go, I was battling with second place.

We went side by side through turns four and five. He was on the inside there, and that put him on the outside for six, the next quick 90-degree right hander. Approaching six, he crowded me in from the outside to pinch my entry and exit so he could pass me down the next straight. This was an old-age and treachery move that John Heinricy would teach me again much later at Grattan.

Just before turn in, second place got a little too close and accidentally bumped me. My two right-side tires went onto the grass just before the brake zone. When I hit the brakes, the car went sideways and didn't slow much at all. The inside curbing at six was high and dug out on the backside. The fast way through for some cars is straddling the curb.

As the car slid left and then right towards the corner, the right wheels hit the inside of the curb. Hard. The Civic hopped once, went way up on two wheels, and then rolled slowly onto its roof. I slid all the way across the track and into the gravel trap upside down. The windshield broke in towards me as the car dug in.

I hung in my belts, upside down, pinned to the seat by gravel packed in all around my helmet. As we all do that first time we are upside down, I popped my belts and immediately got caught up in the pedals. I didn't have much room to maneuver with all the gravel above me. When I finally got out, I looked back at the car.

Poor Civic, laying there with all four wheels up in the air.

We put the battered car on the trailer and headed home. The car was badly hurt and I was pretty disappointed. The front frame rails were bent down and most of the front of the car would have to be replaced. The team advised me to scrap the chassis and start over.

Replacement chassis were pretty inexpensive at the time, but it was the first race car I had ever purchased and I was pretty attached. So, I had it fixed. I probably spent more money at the body shop getting the frame pulled and front fixed than I would have done transferring the go-fast parts to a new shell.

As is often the case in racing, the challenge provided an opportunity. In this case, it was changing my paint scheme. Wade and I were the only two racing for Mayhem in 1994, with Mark taking the year off and Tom going out on his own. I decided I would paint my car in the same scheme as his—white with a blue slash. Team cars. Weeks later, the car came back from the body shop in beautiful metallic blue and white with large Mayhem-style yellow numbers on the sides and hood.

It's a paint scheme that I use on all my race cars to this day. Now, I swap the white for bright yellow, but the design has otherwise stayed the same.

One of my favorite pictures of us as the Mayhem Racing Team is from Blackhawk later that summer. The two blue and white team cars point at each other and the whole team is lined up behind them. For me, it was all about being a part of the team.

BRAND AS SHORTHAND

We've spent quite a bit of time defining our club racing brand and now it's time to execute that brand. This is the care and feeding portion of branding. We've touched on this in each of the previous chapters as we defined the core elements of your club racing brand. I want to talk specifically now about how consistency will help you grow your brand's footprint and reach.

It's easy to think of this visually at first. Each visible element of your brand—voice, character, personality, goals, and purpose—all benefit from consistency. We use brand as a shorthand, or as a symbol or an impression that helps us navigate without researching. In our everyday lives, we know what an established brand stands for and we learn what a new brand stands for. When brands are consistent in their elements over time, it makes it easy for us to trust and position those brands in our minds.

Let's think of visual signals and how branded teams set themselves apart from unbranded ones. Whether it's the guy in the black Jimmy John's polo, the Orkin man in his white shirt, or the red Lowe's or orange Home Depot apron, they are all letting us know who they are and what they do. The consistent theme, color, and presentation are all part of the branding of the organization. We use those visual cues as a shorthand for each brand.

Think UPS and you see the brown truck. Think FedEx and you see the white, logoed truck. Or, Orkin and the red diamond. The list of easily recognizable brands is huge and each one cuts through the clutter and becomes a shorthand to help us make decisions. We don't need to do research on FedEx or UPS, but we might want to look into Bob's Delivery Service to figure out what their customers say before using them.

This is the reason so many brands have opened stores on Amazon. We trust known brands to fulfill our orders much more than a seller we haven't heard of. If that's our only option, then again, we have to learn about their company.

So how do you care for and feed your club racing brand so that it becomes a shorthand for your branding elements? Be consistent. Stay true to your brand. Evolve, don't revolve.

Our club race teams are a bit like local service companies. We start out small, yes, but we have the ability to differentiate ourselves through branding. We start off true to our brand elements, and we stay true to our brand elements. We can manage the impressions we leave with our consumers, fans, partners, and followers. We're not being fake. We're just paying attention to how we present ourselves.

Compare these two service companies.

One: A group of guys with consistent color and branding on their shirts show up in their branded work van. You know who's in the driveway by the color and design of their apparel and vehicle. You know what to expect from their service.

Two: A group of guys with jeans and random t-shirts show up in a plain white work van. You're not quite sure who it is that just pulled into the driveway. The timing is right for Bob's plumbing, but is it really Bob?

Both local companies probably do a similar-quality job, but one gives you an impression they have a better handle on it. The second team needs to earn your trust.

Often, well-branded companies can charge more for their services. They can charge a little more for the shorthand and trust as long as they consistently deliver upon it.

The consistency in branding signals that they are successful, knowledgeable, and organized. It's the difference between generic and name brand at the grocery store. We want our club team to become a name brand, and avoid being generic.

Brand consistency is about more than consistent team gear and paddock space, or car and driver uniforms though. It's about consistency of purpose, goals, character, and the rest of our branding elements. This is why I've stressed the You be You portion so many times throughout this book. It is so much easier to be true to yourselves than it is to be true to something that is a stretch for you and the team. By all means, you should strive to move forwards, but evolve your brand to achieve things in line with your own evolution.

Brand consistency helps others know that you will do what you do what you're known for over and over again. Being consistent helps you become a shorthand in your fans/followers/partners' minds. This is the goal for any branding exercise: become a shorthand for your branded elements. Become easy to remember, easy to trust, easy to expect, and easy to believe in. Being consistent with your approach to each element of your brand will help point you towards becoming that shorthand.

NAMES ON THE BACK OF THE BASEBALL JERSEYS, JUST LIKE THE PROS

What do visuals tell us about a brand? Think of that example of the two local service companies above. Each was branded, one was intentional, and one was not. Each gave you a signal, a shorthand with information about their capabilities. Your brain is very good at finding patterns in things and we put things into buckets very quickly as we have so much information to process. It is this process of shortcuts and shorthanding that we want to take advantage of with our visual branding efforts.

We want that first visual impression of our brand to be a true representation of our brand elements (purpose, goals, character, voice, and personality). As we're starting, one way to think about this is: Who do you want to emulate as a brand? Where would you like to see your brand and your team brand in the future?

Let's say that your goal with your brand or your club team brand is to eventually become a professional team. Use the shorthand signals of professionalism to help people understand your brand goals. People understand how professionals dress, act, and speak.

When most people unfamiliar with professional racing see a race car driver being interviewed, they see a driver in a colorful suit in front of a microphone with a logoed baseball hat thanking partners and talking about their race. That's what they know they see. It's right in front of them. It's the shorthand for them that this is a race car driver.

Here's what they *don't know* that they see. They *don't know* that they see a well-thought-out theme and that the driver's suit complements a well-thought-out theme on the car. They don't know that they see a logo designed and sized just for the hat. They *don't know* they're taking in all the signals that this is a professional. People just see it. It becomes a shorthand for race car driver.

So, what is it about this perception that drives that recognition of success and professionalism? We see it all the time. Look at kids' uniforms for travel sports. Names on the back, just like the pros. Coaches wearing windbreakers, just like the pros. Eye black, batting gloves, necklaces—it's all part of that attempt to shift in perspective to be branded as a pro and to give the impression of a pro. It is this perception that drives our judgement more than anything. It is our first impression, our first gut feel of the person who guides our relationship with the brand.

In your sport, look first to the top local teams, then national teams. What brand image do they put forward? What is your perception of them? Why? Look hard at the imagery. Look hard at the things people rarely see like the shoes and the pants, the stuff that offsets the logoed shirts. Did you notice that the team members were wearing the exact same accessories?

The branding is a shorthand, but it's the consistency of the brand that makes the lasting impression. Every time they see you or your brand, you are living your brand elements both actively and passively. We communicate visually with the world around us that our brand stands for X, always stands for X, and always will stand for X.

This consistent application of our branding elements drives and reinforces our brand perception and breathes soul into our club racing brand. This moves us from unbranded service Company Two to branded and professional service Company One. This is the direction we are headed.

BLUE SUNGLASSES

There is a club racer, Tom O'Gorman, who has worked himself up to the professional ranks. As a part of his visual brand, he puts his face in the lower foreground of each of his social media pictures wearing these goofy, blue-rimmed sunglasses. He did this over and over and over, and pretty soon, just through this consistent approach to his personal branding, you knew if you saw a picture with these blue sunglasses, it was Tom O.

I'm not saying that you need to go out and get some blue-rimmed sunglasses. I'm saying that you can build your brand through consistency. Consistency of appearance can seem boring and like a uniform at times, but this branded consistency is what can help your brand gain visibility and presence at the track and off.

Soon, you will indeed start to think of your appearance as a bit of a uniform, your branded uniform. The coolest part of this is that you get to choose what that is. Stay true to your personal brand where it matters and be consistently in the background where it doesn't.

PADDOCK RESEARCH ASSIGNMENT

At first blush, this is a little about "The Look" as people used to say about Roger Penske's Trans-Am and Can-Am teams back in the 70s. Roger Penske wanted his team to present itself in a specific, professional manner; this at a time when corporate sponsors were just coming on the scene and his teams were the most professional looking in the paddock.

Penske's team paid attention to the small things, the details of racing beyond making cars go faster. They dressed in sponsor colors, hauled cars in enclosed semis at a time when most cars were towed on open trailers, fussed over the littlest of things on the cars, and made sure they were clean and well-presented every time at the track. They were really one of the first top-level teams to overtly approach racing as a business and treat it as professionally branded companies treat their own businesses and brands. Thus, they created "The Look."

Make time at your next event to take a walk through the pit and paddock. Specifically look at the front runners in your sport. Sure, they're likely better funded than we are, but look beyond that spend on the giant toter home and evaluate the condition of the equipment, the tools, the cars.

This paddock walk can often be overwhelming, and a little disheartening, as you realize the shocking amount of money spent on tow vehicles and paddock setups at local races. But this paddock walk isn't about spending more money to get noticed. It's more of an exercise in looking deeply at what others are doing and seeing if there is anything that you can adopt to build your own presence at the track.

Let's get started with understanding how the top competitors do it. Even though we don't have a huge budget, we do have creativity and drive. This'll work just fine. Time for some homework. It's both harder and simpler than you think.

So, as you wander through the paddock at your local track, think about what you're seeing. Who has "The Look" and why?

What looks professional, impressive, or memorable at your local or regional track?

- Is it memorable for the right reasons or the wrong ones?
- Is it the pit space well-planned and organized?
- Are the tow vehicle and trailer clean and presentable?
- Are the awning or pop-up tents well thought out?
- Is the race car clean and straight?
- Do the colors match the car or the main sponsor?
- Is the approach to branding consistent?
- When the crew works on the car, what logos do you see on the backs of their shirts?
- Are they consistent in their placement of their team logo, their sponsor logos, and their series logos? Or, is it sponsor soup?

As you think about how your perception was managed by each team's brand consistency, intentionally or not, let's consider how we can bend some of these ideas to our will. We'll need some marketing tools, but with a little background, we can deliver a carefully crafted brand perception.

In a pro team we see consistency of dress, logo placement, and color scheme. It is this consistency that drives our perception of a team. Just like any sports team, amateur or otherwise, brand consistency guides outsiders' perception.

This approach to branding drives the perception of a team, ours, and others. It is the consistency of branding that catches our attention. It's not the specific brands, but the cohesive, consistent branding of the team presentation.

BE MEMORABLE

As we build our club racing brand, both personal and team, we are building a legacy. It sounds grand, but it is this history and consistent approach to branding that builds a shorthand for partners, followers, and fans. We give them the framework and consistently meet expectations for the brand to the point that they don't even have to think about who we are and what we stand for. They expect us to be us.

We deliver on the elements of our brand and stay consistent in the delivery and execution of our brand. More than anything, it is this consistency that drives a lasting impression of our brand and our team.

As you progress in club racing, especially if your goal is to transition into higher levels of the sport, this brand recognition can open doors. Brand consistency helps you by giving your conversations a head start as the get-to-know-you portion of the conversation has been partially handled by the consistency of your brand. Oh, we know XYZ brand, they're always doing ABC.

This opening comfort level goes a long way with followers, fans, and partners as you've taken a bit of the workload off their shoulders through effective and consistent branding efforts. You've given them shorthand to sift through all the noise.

If you already have an established brand and decide it isn't conveying the right message, you may want to modify it. However, think about brands that changed their logo and how initially jarring it was as you adjusted to the new signal. Before you create a new brand or modify your existing brand, I want you to think hard about all the effort you've put into this brand and know that for some of your fans, followers, and partners, a brand change can mean the elimination of a known shortcut.

You will end up doing a lot of the same branding work over again with that same precise focus you had the first time around. Before you make a brand change, make sure you are committed to building it up and supporting it with a consistent approach. If you commit to the change, be committed to creating a consistent brand that will become a shortcut for your fans, followers, and partners.

Think of race teams that change sponsors and liveries every year, and compare them to the Turner BMW's white, yellow, and blue; the Birel Kart red and white; the Castrol livery of John Force; or the blue of the Subaru Rally Team. All of these are quick and consistent shorthand brand signals for you as a fan.

This focus on brand consistency is not easy. It takes time and patience, and it takes resilience and belief. You don't create a shorthand overnight. This is why we focused on the elements of branding first and didn't jump right into team colors and logos and all the periphery that surrounds branded racers and teams.

All of that stuff is great, but the soul of the brand and the execution of all your branded elements rely heavily on you putting your best effort forward on creating, developing, and refining those six brand elements. Then you need to deliver them with a consistent approach across each.

The core element of your brand is its soul, and if you are true and consistent with your six elements, the visuals become a bit of a dress-up suit. It's okay to change it out from time to time, but your brand has to stay with its you-be-you core, or your fans, followers, and friends will get lost.

The next section of this book will help you speak the language of design and help you amplify the work you've done building the six elements of your brand. More than anything, this next section will help you push towards that branded shorthand for your club racing brand.

This is where we get into what everybody thinks of when they hear the word branding. The shiny new stuff, the logos, and the visual language of your brand.

PART II

HOW TO APPLY BRANDING TO YOU AND YOUR RACING TEAM

8

TEAM NAMES

It's 1996. I've decided to take a break from racing.

Spring and summer were focused on road racing. Fall was rally. Winter was ice racing. After two full years on the four-season racing program and the CRX crash, I needed a break. For me, there was no off-season, so there was no recovering going on. We all need the off-season to recover financially and mentally, but mostly financially!

I crewed for the Buffum Hyundai Rally Team for a couple of rallies in 1995 and 1996. There, I met Hyundai Motorsports Marketing Manager Toni Honzowicz. I also met Troy Lee of Troy Lee Designs. Troy Lee was racing one of the Tiburons. His relationship with HotWheels and the power of his personal brand made a lasting impression on me.

Although I didn't know it at the time, I was building my personal marketing and branding library. Toni had a super-interesting job as motorsports marketing manager. I had no idea that job existed! It was something to think about for the future.

I looked at the other rally cars and saw their partner branding was obscured by mud and dirt after just a few stages. Little things caught my attention, like branding on the roof of the cars, a place that rarely got dirty. The simplicity of the Hyundai brand stood out. It was a large Hyundai logo and Hyundai spelled out with "Rally Team USA" underneath. Hyundai's rally program reinforced the impression of Hyundai's toughness. If their sports cars could survive rally, then they could surely survive everyday roads.

My experience with the rally team and chatting with Toni and Troy set me on the path towards marketing. I knew what I wanted: it was marketing and marketing for a car company. I went back to school and got my MBA. When I graduated, I started in the Marketing Leadership Program at Ford.

Throughout my time at Ford, I learned the art and science of brand marketing. I learned how to tell stories with images, how to make data sing, how to build brands from the ground up, and how to feed a great brand like Mustang.

I was privileged to work with amazing marketing leaders whose passion and vision inspired me. Robert Parker, Jim Farley, Mark Fields, Theo Benson, Paul Anderson, and Vivian Palmer all had and shared clear insight into how to get things done while remaining passionately committed to the customer.

In 2017, after ten years in marketing at Ford, I had a strong feel for brands and brand perception. All of this stocked my mental library when I jumped back into racing. However, even with all this branding background, I made a mistake that a lot of club racers make.

I named my team after myself. Fritz Wilke Racing.

At first it was awesome, picking out a logo, fonts, and all the other details I love. It was all about me. All about my ego. But now that it's become a brand in and of itself, I realize the limitations that I put on my team brand by choosing my own name. Everyone on the team works for Fritz. This is so different than everyone working on the Flying Ghost Racing team or Ollie Rocket Racing team.

I didn't realize that I was building a brand around one driver. This made expanding the team beyond me difficult. We all have egos and we all want to be the front man. It's funny how your ego can get in your way sometimes. One of my favorite Douglas Adams quotes from *The Hitchhikers Guide to the Galaxy* is from one of his most self-centered characters. "If there's anything more important than my ego around, I want it caught and shot now."

It was all about me and that was ok. Now that we've expanded the team, I realize that my brand should be a part of the overall team brand. As a drag racing team, this would have been a perfect approach as one driver is the focus of the whole team. For road racing, karting, and circle track, the dream is often that of a multi-car team.

I was so ready to apply my brand knowledge to my racing that I let my ego get the best of me. It's a lesson I've used to build Flying Ghost and Ollie Rocket. I've loved being more effective the second and third time around. Sometimes, I wish I had started with Ollie Rocket or Flying Ghost, but I know that making mistakes with FWR first made both of those brands stronger.

The marketing and branding lessons I learned on those northern forest roads with John Buffum, Toni Honzowicz, Troy Lee, and Hyundai Rally Team USA were the nudge that pushed me towards marketing and branding. Those simple lessons have stuck with me and I've used them more often than I can remember.

KNOW YOUR BACKSTORY—
SOMEBODY WILL ASK YOU

Your team brand name is all about creating an initial and lasting brand perception. Now that you understand some branding basics, we're ready to move on to the soul of your brand. The soul of your brand is so much more important than the actual name. Remember, with Ford Raptor, as long as the name wasn't overtly dumb, just about anything would have worked because the soul of the brand was so strong.

Before choosing a name, I want you to do the same thing for your brand. Use the six elements of branding to create your own version of running the Baja

1000 with your brand so that naming becomes an easy next step and not a painful, who-do-we-want-to-be kind of exercise.

What do you want people to perceive about your racing team name based on the team name alone? Without any other brand signals? As we saw with Raptor, the accomplishments gave the brand name its foundation and a portion of its soul.

The naming part can often be the most difficult and sometimes least thoroughly explored method of driving brand perception. Your own personal You be You will drive your brand name.

For you as a personal brand, it's easy—it's typically your name. However, you don't have to use your name as your personal brand, especially if it's hard to spell or super common. You can explore other options. If you're in this situation, you can use many of the team branding ideas that follow to create your personal brand.

Your team brand is different. As you consider various brand names for your team, you're building a legend, a backstory, and an entity. Your brand name is going to be one more part of the branded experience that you bring to life.

Let's take Fritz Wilke Racing, for example. It tells you who it is and it's super recognizable among friends. But, if Fritz Wilke is the main driver for Fritz Wilke Racing, it begs the question: Who's the rest of the team? Is there a rest of the team? We're dealing in perception here and we want to put the best foot forward we can.

Be careful of using your full name in your team brand. Think about your circle of friends: Will they be excited to wear gear with your name on their chest or back? There are benefits and drawbacks to using your name. Racing is a family sport after all.

Certainly, there are examples that work like Chip Ganassi, Jac Haudenschild, and Joe Gibbs, who all use their full names. But, until your personal brand becomes larger and more well-known, using your full name typically has more drawbacks than benefits early on. I recommend against using your full name as your first team brand name. It's a mistake I made early on. I eventually shortened it to FWR.

There are exceptions to using your name; one that comes to mind quickly is drag racing as mentioned before. It is common and effective for drag racers to use their whole name as the team name. This is because there is usually only one driver who is also the face and driving force behind the team. In drag racing, it's me vs. you and the competitor is both the team brand and the personal brand. If you are in drag racing, your full name is a very solid option.

Here's an alternative: you can use your last name as part of your team brand. This is a tried-and-true team branding technique. Roush, Penske, Shelby American. You enhance your personal branding without the subtle baggage of your full name. It is a family sport and many families use their last name as their brand name. Typically, these are brands like Rogers Racing, Davis Autosport, Larson Racing, that kind of thing. These work well, and can be leveraged effectively. One thing to be careful of, though, is if your last name is also a relatively common last name, as this can lose a little impact. Smith Racing—which Smith? Jones Racing—which Jones?

Using your last name is tried and true but can be sub-optimal in some instances for the same reasons we talked about for using your whole name. Many club teams do it though, so let's take a look at ways to optimize it. You can research a bunch of themes on the racing part of the name.

Let's use mine. The simplest form is "Wilke Racing". Pretty basic, gets the point across, but it won't stand out from the other XYZ Racing names out there. There are other options.

- **Wilke Autosport**—conveys a European vibe for our road racing team.

- **Wilke Competition**—if we wanted to be different, just to be different, or maybe to be perceived as a race team and shop.

- **Wilke Speedsports**—a similar vein to Wilke Competition.

- **Team Wilke**—if we were going for a bigger team feel. On my personal brand, we use Team FWR, so that can be an option later.

The variations are many. You can add in the form of motorsport before racing too. Such as Wilke Road Racing, Wilke Karting, or Wilke Rally Team. Each of these leans on family. If family is a significant part of your You be You, then this is an excellent way to go. Just be aware of the limitations you are placing on yourself as using your last name may not have the reach you hope for at first.

Here are some other brand words to think about pairing with your last name: Motorsports, Racers, Performance, Race Team, or Racing Team.

Ok, so there are other options, of course. The third and likely best option is to come up with something new. There are so many choices! There isn't an easy trick for picking a brand name for your team. So, how do you narrow it down?

Well, it helps to have some alternatives to look at before you dive in. I suggest, if you haven't already, taking a look at one of the many endurance racing series team pages. Browse through the hundreds of teams listed there. It can get the creative juices flowing. Here are some specific guidelines that can help you as you look to create your team's name.

Don't copy somebody else's team name; be original. After all, your brand is original, it has a soul, and we need to name it properly. One of the best parts of this process is when you find that name that works and you know how you got there, the backstory presents itself and the next time you're asked, you can answer the question about the origin of the team name.

Tie your brand name back to your brand elements. What's your purpose, character, personality, goals, and voice, and how are you consistent? Each answer gives you a little nudge towards your name. This isn't easy and it often helps to run your options by friends who you trust will tell you the truth.

Come up with at least three name options before choosing one. That third option makes the choice less binary, and you tend to see a little more of what you like and what you don't like in each option.

Time for nuts and bolts. How do we actually pick a name that lasts, speaks to our brand, and represents us?

BLEEDING EDGE FLAMING SWORD DROP RACING

Heads up: here come some marketing tricks for creating brand names. At first, it seems a little odd that people have thought about this stuff, but they have and it works. I've been part of naming quite a few branded things in my career and you'd be amazed at the power of things like syllables in a brand name.

Sometimes, a naming strategy is part of a corporate mission to deliver consistency, as at Ford where all the sedans needed to start with an F and the SUVs start with an E. It was a big deal when Flex broke with this tradition. The break was on purpose to position the Flex as a wagon instead of an SUV in the minds of Ford marketers and customers. Ford follows this naming convention around the world on SUVs and sedans, except for pickups and the Icons—Mustang, Raptor, GT, and Bronco. Yep, those are called the Icons at Ford.

Other times, the brand name just needs to roll off the tongue when combined with the corporate brand.

Sometimes names stand on their own. You know lots of these examples. Think of a few from your world that work and those that don't.

As strange as it may seem, the way people say a brand name impacts the perception of that brand. Combination names are easy to remember and easy to say. Try to keep the number of syllables even across the two names or think of the syllables as a rhythm. The fewer syllables in the second word, the better. *Da da dum. Da da dum.*

Examples:

- Fly-ing Liz-ard
- Bim-mer World
- Gas Mon-key Gar-age
- Act-ion Ex-press
- Drag-on Speed
- Oll-ie Rock-et
- A-tom-ic Squir-rel
- Fly-ing Ghost

When you make your brand name easy to say, you make it easy to remember. It's important to think about ease of use when you want someone else to talk about your brand. Make it easy for them to say your name to someone else. Make it easy for your friends, fans, partners, and followers to talk about your brand to their friends.

This builds your brand in small ways. When a corporate team evaluates your proposal against others, if yours is easy to say and easy to remember, it'll be easy for them to communicate as they pitch you over the competition. Flying Lizard Racing will probably win the name recognition game over Bleeding Edge Flaming Sword Drop Racing. Although the latter is a pretty cool name, it'll get shortened to "Bleeding something something" in the partner's office.

If you want to be taken seriously, stay away from puns or vulgar language. Bouncing TaTas Racing might have been hilarious when you came up with it at the bar, but, when you have to go in front of a group of corporate people or a small business seeking a partnership, a name like that can make some companies nope right out. Those partners you talk to have to sell their bosses on this and if they snicker or are embarrassed to say a team name, it becomes much easier to pass you by for someone or something else a little less complicated. Think about losing a bet and having to tell your friend's grandma your team name.

However, if a funny or vulgar name is the direction you want to go, then think about the companies who would think it is just as funny as you do and pivot to pursuing them as partners. There's no wrong way here. You don't have to be corporate vanilla. It's just a matter of how you want to manage the perception of yourself and your team. Think of it as opening some doors while closing others.

TIE IT BACK TO YOUR YOU BE YOU

Use your brand name to tell a story: *your* brand story. Every part of a brand name comes with a story. So, what will your tale be? What's your You be You. What is it that moves you?

You love being on stage, so Bright Lights Racing? You love the outdoors, so Hidden Trail Racing? You love being in the water, so Slippery Nipple Racing? Wait, no. How about Ocean's Crest Racing? You love winning, so Flying Cork Racing? You are grassroots to the core, so Grass Paddock Motorsports? Maybe your You be You is all about being from da region where you grew up, so Molten Steel Racing, I-Beam Racing, or Blast Furnace Racing become contenders.

Know the backstory, know why you chose your brand name. You'll be asked, so you should think through how you will tell the story. "I thought it was a cool name" misses an opportunity to engage your audience. It can leave them flat and won't showcase the personality driving the brand. You want the backstory for your brand name to be one that people will tell. It helps breathe a little more life into your brand.

Each example above begs the story question, "Why did you choose that as your team name?" That's your cue to give the backstory, to load their lips as they talk about you and spread the word about your team brand. This kind of storytelling gives life and strength to brands.

This process can be much more fun than intimidating. When I asked my eight-year-old son, Will, what he wanted his team name to be, he looked at his cat, Oliver, and said Ollie Racing. When I asked him to describe Ollie, he said he takes off like a rocket! I asked if we should add that in and he loved it. Ollie Rocket Racing was born.

Sometimes you can come up with so many good ideas you get lost. Thrift it down to a list of three or four great candidates, know each backstory, and see which ones speak to you and your team.

Why did we choose Flying Ghost Racing Team for our endurance team brand? We love the road racing team Flying Lizard, so it's an homage of sorts to one of our favorite teams. Why Flying Ghost? Well, we're fast, we sneak up on you, but we're also approachable and fun.

We added in Easter eggs in our Flying Ghost branding to tell a broader story with our endurance brand. An image of the Wisconsin and Indiana flags speaks to the heritage of the team's founders, Jasper and me. The yellow and blue reflects my long-time racing colors. The fireball logo has sunglasses and a smirk that speaks to our sense of humor.

I have found that picking the team name and building a story helps guide me later when picking or designing the team logo and colors. Ollie Rocket Racing is a unique one, however.

When I asked Will what he wanted his logo to be, he immediately responded, "An Octopus." When asked why, he replied, "I don't know, I just want it to be an octopus." Okay, then. It sure made things easier by narrowing the imagery down so early!

Find the name that connects with your You be You, the soul of this brand you've created. Pick it from a group of three or four choices, run them by friends and family, have a naming contest, and see what people like and why. At the end of the process, make your own decision and stick with it.

9
LOGOS

It's late summer 2008 and I'm in a conference room just down the hall from my 9th floor office at Ford's Regent Court.

I was listening to the first pitch of the 2010 Mustang Reveal from our partners at the agency. It was the first refresh since 2004, so we were going big with the reveal. We'd redesigned the Mustang Pony logo to be more sharp-edged to communicate that modern take on an icon. The Pony logo redesign was a signal for the direction the car was supposed to go.

Unfortunately, while we'd sharpened up the Pony, we'd gone quite conservative with the design of the actual car. There wasn't much change. We needed to do something else to create interest in a car that, frankly, was a mild update.

To solve this problem, we built a 12-week tease campaign. It would conclude the week before the reveal. We released images each week, starting with the front of the car, working to the back and into the interior. The goal of the campaign was to annoy the journalists. Why?

We wanted them to say, "Enough already! Show us the damn car!" as opposed to showing the whole car at the reveal and getting a collective, "Meh, not much change there."

We thought it'd be about six weeks before we got the journos annoyed and we weren't far off. Complaints came in strong at week eight and beyond.

Every time somebody said, "Show us the damn car!" we knew our plan was working. That was the whole point. We wanted people to want to see the new car.

We were revealing the Mustang at Barker Hanger in Los Angeles on the eve of the 2008 LA Autoshow. We had a stage set up like an arena with an arc of grandstands across the front. Once the audience was seated, Vaughn Gittin, Jr. would bring his new 2010 drift Mustang onto the stage followed by the 2010 production Mustangs.

As a backdrop to the stage, we were highlighting Mustang's broad motorsports heritage. We had legendary IMSA, NHRA, and Trans-Am cars stacked up on racks on each side of a central video screen. Each car had a famous driver associated with it and they were all there for the reveal. Twelve racing legends, including Jack Roush and Carroll Shelby, were there alongside Jim Farley, then head of marketing at Ford.

In the original plan, a C-5 Galaxy would fly in and taxi to the hangar. The cars would come down the plane's ramp with lots of smoke and flashing lights. Unfortunately, that was way out of our budget. The advertising agency's alternative was to have the seats of the arena just high enough off the floor for the Mustangs to slide out from underneath them and into the arena we'd created.

The pitch had a lot of hyperbole from the agency—never been done! First of its kind! When the agency team described their plan for a video of the car on the main screen as it came out from under the stands as a never-been-done moment, I'd had enough.

I pointed out rather directly that this was the intro for just about every sporting event from college to pros. Yes, the concept was awesome, but no, it certainly wasn't the first of its kind.

I earned myself the nickname Fritz of Darkness in that moment. The nickname stuck and agency teams were leery of presenting to me from then on. It was dumb of me really. I liked the idea, I just rejected the hyperbole. I should have just let it go.

We used the idea—it was a great idea at its core and the reveal went amazingly well. People loved the car and gushed about how cool the evening's entertainment was. Vaughn drifting into the arena with Mark Fields in the passenger seat was awesome!

To this day, that over-the-top reveal at Barker Hanger in the fall of 2008 remains one of my favorite memories of my time at Ford. Fritz of Darkness or not. And all of it started with that redesign of the Pony logo and our plan to bring the past into the future.

DOWN THE RABBIT HOLE WE GO

This is my favorite bit of the whole process, so bear with me. In this next section, we're going to get you ready to pick a design or have a conversation with a designer to get your logo made.

We talked about building the story of your team name. Now, it's time to connect the words with a symbol for your team. Let's start simple, using the words of your team name as the brand.

We'll use Ollie Rocket Racing for an example. When we write it out, it looks like this:

Ollie Rocket Racing

We have lots of options for presenting our team name as our brand. Let's try stacking it, adding dots on either side of "Racing", and making it all caps:

OLLIE ROCKET
• RACING •

If you're going this route, this is the time to choose a font. Fonts are split into serif, which have little dangly bits on each letter that are made for body text, and sans-serif, which are made for titles and do not have the dangly bits. It's the difference between **Times New Roman** and **Helvetica**. See the dangly bits on Times New Roman?

Pick three or four racing brands whose fonts resonate with you. Does their style fit with your brand?

How about using an acronym of your team name. For example, Fritz Wilke Racing becomes FWR.

Try this.

- Do a Google image search for your team's acronym.
- Copy the logos that catch your eye. Select about a dozen or so.
- Weed out the ones you don't like. Save them though, we'll use them in a bit.
- Print out the top five in grayscale. This eliminates color from the decision-making process.
- Place them on the wall and step back to see them as a design.
- Pick four from this group and pick four from the group you discarded. Put all eight on the wall.
- Make notes on each logo about what you like and what you don't.

This process will help you see the letters as a brand and clarify what resonates with you and your team's brand. This is a good starting point for your logo as an acronym. Now it's time to connect with a designer.

DON'T BE FRITZ OF DARKNESS

Don't do it. I'm telling ya, it's not a good idea.

Be patient and listen. When you meet with the graphic designer for the first time, bring your image packets and your brand elements. This will help them get a clear understanding of the soul of your brand. They can interpret your brand's vision alongside your image packets.

One of the contradictory things that drives graphic designers crazy is too much freedom. It seems odd, but the more open ended you make the start of the project, the longer it will take. When you don't give them up-front guidance, you are asking them to trial and error their way into direction. This isn't efficient.

It's important to find a common language of design. Figure out what you like and don't like and communicate it. Remember how we all interpret who or what an architect is differently when we don't have a frame of reference to rely on. I use this idea to help guide my designers. I find three or four designs that highlight my idea or theme. It helps the designer understand what I'm trying for.

Most graphic designers will take the proactive step of asking you to bring design ideas to the first meeting. They want to deliver a product they're proud of in a reasonable amount of time and with a reasonable effort. Be kind to your designer. Even though it is your logo, it is their art and they want to be proud of their creation.

How do you find a designer? First, look at racing team logos you like and reach out to the team for a contact. The designer they used will already have worked with a race team, so they'll have a step up on one who hasn't. Ask to take a look at their portfolio. Is there anything you like? Not all designers and clients are a good fit. Make sure they like to do the type of logo you want. If you want a pizza, you don't go to Taco Bell. You can go on sites like Fiverr and 99designs to connect with freelancers as well.

Try to find a designer who you can meet with in person or is at least willing to videoconference. You will at some point want to move some bit just a little to the left and delete that bit over there, so you need to ask questions in real time. These conversations are far more effective when you're both looking at the art.

Price ranges for design services can be quite broad. Make sure you understand how many changes and meetings you are entitled to and how you can modify the agreement. Make sure you understand delivery dates and deadlines. Your logo isn't the only project the designer is working on. You will find that whatever limits you put on yourself that first time, you'll exceed them. Understand the fees and timing for changes ahead of time. This isn't their first rodeo, they'll help you. Once you've developed that relationship, you'll be amazed at the level of help you will receive.

You will want to secure your logo in multiple versions so you can use it on a variety of surfaces and backgrounds. Ask for multicolor, black and white, and tone-on-tone versions. Even if you don't think you'll use them, ask for the design files. Printers, designers, and other artists will ask for them if you need embroidery, stickers, ads, or a website created. Work with your designer to optimize this from the beginning. Ask them to provide you with brand guidelines, specifying how your logo looks and how different versions should be used.

BRANDING SPEED

A designer who has been with you from the start can mold your design into many, many applications.

MODERN WITH A TOUCH OF DARKNESS

If you've chosen to pursue a symbol for your team, repeat the search engine steps you did with the acronym, but use your team name and add the word logo. Let's focus on the images it returns. Get a feel for what fits the image of your brand.

Here's the process we used for both Flying Ghost and Ollie Rocket. For Ollie Rocket, we already knew what type of brand we wanted, so we searched for octopus logos. Everything from goofy to scary came up. We selected four candidates that said modern with a touch of darkness. We found the theme we liked through these four and narrowed down to this logo that resonated.

This logo was available for commercial use on Shutterstock. We paid the fee for the rights and sent it over to our local graphic designer friend, Heather

Heiderer. She said she could make a few tweaks to make it our own and we were off to the races!

We simplified the logo to work online, in print, and on apparel. We got one logo and many uses, without change. That made it easier for our vinyl and apparel suppliers. Next, we finalized the font for the letters for Ollie Rocket Racing. We chose a modern font because it fit with our brand.

For Flying Ghost, we'd already been through both the FWR and Ollie Rocket design process. We repeated the logo search and we found a logo that we loved right away—almost too much. Nothing seemed to measure up to this awesome example we had found.

I had misread the description of the logo. It was already in use by a brand. Not only that, it had been created through a logo contest and they were super proud of it. We decided that we didn't want to pay to license it. Many logo owners are open to licensing their logo, but some are not. If they do say no, please don't use it without their permission. You'll likely receive a cease and desist letter.

We restarted the whole process. We went through the weeding-out process and landed on one image that was in our original set of ten logo choices. It was a fireball wearing what looked like sunglasses.

We purchased the rights to use it commercially. It needed a lot of help from Heather. She gave suggestions on how we could bring the logo forward a bit and make it more impactful. The fireball's sunglass eyes got a bit larger and changed shape slightly. She added the trademark smirk and massaged the ghost shape a bit and our Flying Ghost Fireball was born. This process took several weeks of back and forth.

MARIGOLD AND TWO SHADES OF BLUE

Logo development can be a little chicken and egg. Do you pick your team colors and then your logo? Or pick your logo and add your colors later? It's really whatever works best for you. I like picking the shape and then adding the colors later. Team colors are part of the brand name, brand logo, and brand colors. All three are intertwined.

How do you pick team colors? Here are some simple tricks. Take your favorite color, find a color that complements it, add in one or two accent colors, and you're done. Really, it's that simple to start off.

Colors do have meaning, so it helps to understand the image different colors project. Here are six colors and the meanings they convey. Red symbolizes action, passion, energy, and strength. Orange is optimistic, enthusiastic, and youthful. Yellow is fun, warm, and happy. Green is safe, harmonious, and natural. Blue is confident, purposeful, and powerful. Purple is artistic, mysterious, and royal.

When choosing multiple colors, it's helpful to consult the color wheel. The primary colors are red, blue, and yellow. To get the secondary colors, purple, green, and orange, combine the primaries. Everything else is shades in between these six colors. Primaries are always opposite secondary colors on the wheel. Red is opposite green. Yellow is opposite purple. Blue is opposite orange. These pairs are complementary colors and they make for striking design.

There are tertiary colors that can act as accents for each of the primary or secondary colors. The tertiary colors include yellow-orange, yellow-green, blue-green, blue-purple, red-purple, and orange-red. Each of these complements other tertiary colors.

Choose your main color first. It doesn't have to be red, blue, or yellow. Then pick complementary colors. If you find that the colors don't show up well next to each other, consider a darker, more contrasting color as an outline. For instance, white doesn't show up well on yellow. The tones are too close and the eye blurs them together, but if you add a dark outline to the white, it pops.

This happened with the Gulf livery used on the Ford GT40s at LeMans. Gulf Oil's colors were originally dark blue and marigold. Grady Davis, a Gulf VP and a racer himself, ran a GT40 at Daytona in dark blue and orange. He later asked to use the light blue from one of their subsidiaries, Wiltshire Oil, instead of the dark blue because it was more interesting to him.

After they put the marigold and light blue on the car, something didn't work. There wasn't enough contrast between the colors—they were equiluminant. They had the same visual energy. Where they met, the brain mentally blurred the transition. One of the designers added a thin stripe of the original gulf dark blue between the marigold and light blue to create contrast.

Fast forward to 2018 and we're working with the designers on the new Ford GT Heritage Edition, which was painted in light blue and marigold. The designers wanted to eliminate the stripe. In person, without the stripe, we experienced that same blurring of the colors that they did in the 60s. After a ton of back and forth, a trip to see some of the original cars solved the issue. The original dark blue stripe was retained.

Let's take that lesson and apply it to our race team. The brighter the color, the more saturated it is, the more effective the color will be at standing out. As we saw in the example above, colors with similar saturation placed side by side will need a separator to make them pop.

When working with your logo, it is important that your design and your colors work together to build the image of your brand. There is a reason many logos are two colors or a combination of one color and white or black. That simple contrast focuses on the logo design.

Okay, that's all for normal colors, but what about chrome, Day-Glo, and matte finishes? How do they fit?

Each one should be in your menu when you are choosing a color. Chrome is difficult and expensive to produce in apparel and print, so I recommend staying away from chrome in your logo. Instead, use chrome as an element for your racing paint scheme. On your race car, you can put chrome next to just about any color and it will offset that color. Racers who use chrome typically use it as an accent.

Day Glo or neon colors are another story completely. Day Glo colors were developed by the Switzer Brothers in the 1930s. Their pigments reflected not only visible but also invisible light. These ultraviolet reflections help give the Day Glo colors their depth and intensity.

Day Glo works well for logos, but a word of caution, it is nearly impossible to reproduce Day Glo on screen. Many race cars use fluorescent or Day Glo paints and vinyls in their schemes. The complementary color you use, however, needs to be vibrant enough to stand up to the visual power of Day Glo.

For a logo, I advise using only one Day Glo color. Using more than one Day Glo color reduces the impact—similar to the effect with light blue and marigold. Pink, blue, red, green, and yellow are the primary Day Glo colors. When choosing your Day Glo color, be aware that yellows tend to bend towards green, reds towards pink, and oranges towards red.

This brings us to matte finishes. Matte finishes lack the shiny quality we have come to expect from brands and logos. For a logo, this subtlety can get lost. It's especially difficult online or in print. Matte works best in larger surface coverings. Several race teams have embraced matte finishes for their primary color, but for a logo, matte will struggle to deliver.

ON THE WALL AT SIEBKINS

Let's embrace the purest elements of your logo. Think of your logo in one color, white or black. The basics of the monochrome shape and form will work on any color background. You can use your logo in one of your primary colors, too. Place it on any contrasting background and make it pop.

This is another thing that brand guidelines can help you sort out. Make sure you have the flexibility that you need for all the applications you anticipate. You will need to specify at least three or four monochrome versions of your logo depending on the team colors you choose. Make sure you develop a white and a black version of your logo as well. A one-color format is cheaper and easier to produce for apparel.

Today's vinyl printers are amazing and they can do anything on vinyl; however, print colors are slightly different from online colors. Keep a record of the colors you use in print versus online. Make sure you develop stickers, too. After all, your race team sticker needs to go on the wall at Siebkins.

Apparel is unique. To get the same color impact on apparel, designers use a version of the same colors called process color. You will need to ask your designer to provide these for you if you intend to use your logo on apparel. The more colors you use, the more expensive it will be to screen print or embroider your logo onto apparel. Each color gets its own screen and own ink. This is a manual process and each step in the process costs time and money.

Online applications give you the most flexibility. You can use shading, shadows, color blends, and the full capabilities of screens. You can even have the logo animated if you choose. This is especially useful when you work on video. However, this can also be a rabbit hole. It is very easy to spend a lot of time detailing the online version of your logo because you will see it every day. Have a look at other teams and other brand logos online.

DO YOU WANT TO DO A LOGO CONTEST?

You may be overwhelmed trying to pick the right designer and be tempted to use an online service for a design contest. This can be an easy solution at first, but I've found that it is difficult to describe the logo I want in a one-time brief.

If you do this, your brief will need to specify all the options including multicolor, multiple versions, apparel vs. stickers vs. online, plus logo ownership, rights, and brand guidelines. Once you've built this into your brief, you send it for bid to several dozen designers. Amazing things can indeed happen in this process, but if you want to get amazing work, the bid amount must be sizeable. I recommend against this path unless you have a fair amount of experience writing briefs for logos.

ONLINE LOGO DESIGN SERVICES

I prefer a hands-on approach to design and I appreciate the back and forth that we have with our designer. If time is limited or this just isn't your strong suit, working with a team of freelancers might be for you.

There are a couple of sites that specialize in logos. Fiverr and 99designs both connect freelance designers from around the world with clients. Think of and approach the online freelance design process similar to the way you would approach the in-person process. You'll go through designer's online portfolios just like you would when hiring an in-person graphic designer.

One last word of caution for using online resources for logo design: you will need to ensure you can have commercial rights to them. Sometimes online, people can misrepresent a logo as their own creation when it is really in use and trademarked by someone else. Be careful and verify before you finalize your design.

10

THE RACE CAR AND THE RACING DRIVER

It's 1978 and I'm a fourth grader at Thomas E. Elliott Elementary School.

I went to school for book fair day, carrying my little, rubberized, slotted coin holder. I'd saved up and was determined to find something neat. At the end of the day, they set us free in the library to find the treasures that we would just *have* to take home. What I didn't know is that I would find a poster of Hurley Haywood in his white 935 with flames spitting from the exhaust. At the bottom were the words "Porsche Power!"

I put that poster right next to my bed, high up on the wall, and I looked at it most nights before I fell asleep. I had no idea how the car made fire and why the simple red, white, and blue surrounding the circled 59 resonated so much with me, but it stuck. The way the colors draped over the curves and surrounded the number plate said "race car" to me.

Over time I discovered other race cars and other street cars. Yes, I had a Countach on my wall as a kid. It was black, trimmed with gold with wings, angles, and fat tires. It screamed menace and performance in the same breath.

Today, my son has a picture of Hans Stuck jumping the Nurburgring

Flugplatz in his BMW Batmobile. The livery flows and drapes over the modified 320 and follows each line and crease like it did on the 935.

In 2016, as I designed the livery for my Fiesta, I wanted to either evolve or reflect liveries from my past race cars. I knew how much my yellow and blue Honda stood out. I tried out several themes and colors, but came back to the yellow and blue slash down the sides. In the past, I had left the roof white or yellow. This was my chance to do something interesting with that space. I experimented with geometric shapes before finalizing the triangle motif.

I'd always had painted race cars, but this time I chose to wrap the car to make it easier to repair. It was amazing to see the plain car transformed into brilliant yellow and blue in a matter of hours.

My vinyl guy, a longtime road racer himself, kept asking me if I was sure I wanted the numbers so large. Large numbers are unusual in road racing. They take up space normally reserved for partners. I'm glad I persisted. Those stand-out large numbers have become a key part of the branding of the race car. They're as much a part of the design as the yellow and blue with orange trim has become. Altogether, that package is the #84 car.

As a born and bred Hoosier, I wanted to show respect to my heritage. The State of Indiana logo—the torch and stars—is on the back of my suit and helmet. It's now become a part of my personal brand. I even have the logo on the roof of my car.

When new partners come on board, the overall design stays the same. The partner logos fit into the branded scheme. Each car we've built since the Fiesta has worn the same livery and the presence of our team cars continues to expand.

When I look back to that spring day way back in fourth grade, I didn't know how influential that book fair visit would be. That poster of the 935 spitting fire, chasing down the competition has been the standard by which I judge each one of my race car liveries. More than anything, I think it was the colors and their integration into the shape of the car that stayed with me and continues to inspire me to this day.

BE THE #84 CAR

NASCAR teams are experts in branding every aspect of team and driver, and the number is as much a part of the brand identity as the colors. The large number on the side of the car is a key part of the brand of the race car and driver. Think of #3, #9, #24, #43, or #48. I bet you can put a NASCAR driver name with each of those. That's the power of brand consistency.

For other series, the race number is an afterthought, just there for timing and scoring. Drag racing, rally, endurance racing, and road racing follow this method.

Large numbers on the sides and top of your race car makes it easy to identify, talk about, and point out to friends. When you start to think of large numbers as an integral part of your overall design, then they become a part of your brand. In your sport, have a look around and see if anyone is leveraging this simple trick to becoming more memorable. We've found in our form of road racing that we can stand out with large, bold numbers on the side.

We are the #84 car. The number itself came from the original Mayhem racing team. Mark Utecht was #83 and Tom Schabel was #82. I didn't like the way #81 looked. #84 was a multiple of seven, so it had to be lucky. Us drivers and our superstitions.

I've been #84 for my entire racing career. In each series, I've chosen #84. In most series, you can pay a small fee to reserve your number for the year and you can race with that number all year. In others, you have to get registered super early to make sure to get your number. For karting, it's the same way—register early, reserve your number, and you're good to go.

This feeds into brand consistency. You're always the same number, so you're easy to find. Your goal should be to have the car that the kids remember, the bright one, the one with lots of contrast. At first it may seem like you are using up a lot of real estate with these oversized numbers, but having large, friendly numbers on the side of the car just adds to your brand.

STAND OUT IN A SEA OF COLOR

Okay, we've all seen race cars. Which ones do you remember? Think back to the last race you attended where you had a little time to watch. What caught your eye? What did you see that worked?

First and foremost is likely contrast. Bold colors contrasting other bold colors is highly effective. You don't have to do Day Glo orange to stand out, but think about the boldness of the paint schemes around you.

There are a few tricks that you can use in just about every form of motorsports. Lots of us are constrained by budget, so we'll start with the base color of the car. What can you do with your car in the color it was painted? It's all about contrast here. Let's assume for a moment that your car is already red. What color is your lettering going to be? Red's contrast color is green. White shows up very well on red, too. I did just this with my first race car. I used the large numbers and consistent white decals to differentiate.

You can also use white as a broad accent color. This can be in the form of stripes or large swaths of color. Go online and get a line drawing of your race car. Then, search for the best red race car paint schemes to see what others are doing. Use colored pencils and draw the pattern in. Start with just a little red and keep on adding to see what you can come up with. This is the fun coloring book, so let those creative juices flow!

After round five or six, you'll start coming back to themes you like.

Most details in a paint scheme get lost on the track. Simple color schemes can be super effective. It isn't always about large blocks of color, as simple accents on cars with great lines can be powerful. Tape your line drawings up on a wall and walk at least 10-15 feet away to see how things contrast from a distance.

We learned this lesson with our son's go kart. After spending weeks designing a complicated scheme for his sidepods and Nassau panel, I found the color of his sleeves and his helmet stood out far more than anything else. When the kart was stopped, sure, it was easy to see the design, but that 50-100-yard sightline was all about the sleeve and helmet.

Once you finish your design, think about how you will apply your partner logos. If you have a two-color scheme, the logos will be more powerful in only one color. Use either the body color or white depending on the background.

If you have the budget to do a complete scheme and can change colors as you choose, try this: take a closer look at the color wheel and pair the colors on the opposite sides of the color wheel together for high contrast. Go check out other race car ideas in these colors. Now add in an accent color from the white, black, gray, chrome selection and off you go!

This is all about standing out in a sea of chaos. Being more chaotic can get lost. Sometimes, the simplicity of a two-or three-color livery can amplify the brand message.

CHANGE YOUR MIRRORS

As your club racing team grows from one car to multiple cars, you will start to look at the team presence as a whole. How does each car work together when parked next to each other in the paddock, on grid, etc.?

As a team, you will want to extend your livery and branding across the stable. Team cars in the same livery are a statement of the team brand. Think of F1 cars, for example. Or remember the orange and white RealTime Acuras in the 90s and 2000s. The Gulf GT40s, the Marlboro McLarens, all had brand presence extended over multiple vehicles.

There is a balance between extending the brand and easy identification. When your cars are on track at the same time, your crew and partners will need to tell the individual cars apart. You will want to create an obvious way to help your fans, followers, and partners tell the cars apart, too. Teams are used to differentiating cars, so you have lots of options.

You can use contrasting colors on the mirrors, windshield banner, headlight lenses, side window surrounds, or wing end plates. There are many places that you can change color and not change your paint scheme. Think about what is easiest to pick out as the cars are coming at you. You can go crazy with this, too. Some of the more extreme variations include reversing the colors of the livery, substituting out one color and keeping the rest the same, changing the number color, and adding a contrasting stripe between colors.

CHECK OUT IRACING DESIGNERS!

We're club racers. We spend our money on race cars and race car parts. I remember buying tires instead of a couch for my apartment at one point.

If you're getting stuck, dead-ending on a livery design, what do you do?

Your graphic design team is your ace in the hole. They've made all the color combination mistakes long ago. Ask them for high-contrast, high-visibility colors that will define your brand. You've already worked with them on the logo, so this should be a no-brainer. They may not have experience in race car design, so if they're up for it, awesome! If not, then ask them to help you choose your color combinations.

Ok, let's say they can't help you with the livery. What do you do? Reach out to iRacing designers or racecar livery designers. We use BTCC Blueprints for ours. One of the cool things about using iRacing designers is that they have access to 3D models of your car. Sometimes, the front, back, sides, and top viewed separately doesn't give the same impact as a revolving model of the car.

iRacing liveries are typically $25-100, so the pricing can be very reasonable. Use them for the basic structure of the design. You want to nail this first, then add the numbers and the rest on your own later. If you need help placing partner logos, they can help with that too. But take it in a couple of steps—do the livery first, then the partner logos, and off you go!

VINYL VS. PAINTING

This is a tricky choice for sure. It all depends on your discipline and your anticipation of damage. It's typically about $2,000 to paint the car and the same price for vinyl. One of the reasons I like vinyl over paint is it is much easier to replace a panel or small section than it is to take the car in for a touch-up respray.

As vinyl has become ubiquitous throughout the industry, you can now have the car wrapped in a printed vinyl livery that contains all your logos. In club racing, this may not be worth the extra time and money required to create a design like this. Sometimes it's just easier to have a main design and add in partner logos later.

Paint, on the other hand, gives you a depth and sheen not quite possible yet with vinyl. With paint, you can play with the amount of metal flake, the amount of pearl, and the depth of the clearcoat that you cannot with vinyl. Paint is certainly more expensive the more colors you choose and the more intricate the design. This is where vinyl trumps paint by quite a lot. However, a well-painted car almost always stands out better than a wrapped one. Vinyl is getting more and more awesome, but paint gives a perception of depth in sunlight that vinyl can't quite do. Yet.

This is a little about budget and a little about time, both initial and repair. If you have easy access to a body shop, your decision skews a little towards painting the car. If you don't, then typically vinyl is the most cost-effective method of creating your vision of the paint scheme.

WHITE WHEELS

Sometimes when everybody is different, it all becomes the same in its difference. If everybody uses a unique windshield banner, then your unique windshield banner doesn't mean quite as much. However, if everybody has the same color hood as the rest of the livery and we go with matte black, we stand out. If everybody has a plain roof and we do graphics up there, we stand out. If no one has vinyl on the rear windows and we add a small, visible element there, we stand out. As you look at your specific club series, find out what these differentiators are and how you can stand out from a distance.

For us, a simple example is this: we use white wheels on the race car. It's for two purposes. The first is practical. It's super easy to see a crack in a white wheel vs. a black or silver wheel. The second is branding. We stand out from the sea of silver and black wheels with our distinctive white wheels. It's about being visually different.

Take some time and see the racecars as a whole field. Find those simple things that others are not doing and apply some of those things to your car. Most of the time, this is a simple and inexpensive way to help your race stand out from the pack.

IT'S HOT OUT THERE

Here's another way to have fun with branding: brand yourself. This doesn't just mean cover your suit with your partner logos. It means incorporate the team color scheme. You don't need to go out and buy a new suit to do this, but, when you're ready for that next suit or gloves, get them in the same color family as the car and team.

Put your team logo on your suit. Suit embroidery is surprisingly reasonable. It does take time though, and it can be six weeks from shipping your suit out to getting your suit back. If you have a two- or three-layer suit, ask them to remove the lining, use Nomex thread, and sew just through the top layer. You don't want to compromise the suit's effectiveness.

There are other techniques like dye sublimation and vinyl transfer. What you choose depends on your suit's composition. Go with a race car suit decorator. There are many out there. It's best to do this in the late fall when your season's completed and you have a gap to the next year.

Now, think of what you wear around the paddock. Are you always in a t-shirt getting dirty working on the race car? Awesome, let's work with that. Find a crew shirt you can brand and that is resilient—maybe black or dark gray. Put your logo on it and wear that when you're at the track.

Or, are you more of a schmoozer who wanders the paddock talking with everybody? Then maybe go for a polo shirt or a dri-fit that has your logo on it.

These are relatively inexpensive and easy to create once you've sorted out colors and logo. The point is, you are living your brand with every interaction. Think about how you want people to remember you.

If you are in a series that requires Nomex underwear under your suit, then brand it. Make sure you have it branded with your team logo and your partner logos. Why? Because when we get out of the car, we all take our arms and shoulders out of that sleeping bag of a driver's suit and tie it around our waist.

If we have plain Nomex underwear under our suits, all of our partner and team logos are tucked away at the waist. To do this, go with the same race suit company. Ask for water-based ink, so it's not flammable. Put the same team or partner logos on your chest and back. You can even brand the sleeves if you choose. This way, when your suit is around your waist, the partners you represent are right there on your chest and back.

11

PERSONAL BRAND AND RACING TEAM BRAND

It's 2014 and I'm Fiesta Marketing Manager.

I was sent to the Minneapolis Auto Show to represent the brand. It was there I first found out what it was to be branded as a corporate guy.

I was easily dismissed. My statements and opinions were viewed through the lens of a corporate guy. I'd hear comments like, "*You're just the Ford guy, of course you would say that.*" These interactions actually honed my speaking skills. To bring a little neutrality to my public speaking, I had to find examples where I could compare and contrast in both positive and negative ways. This reinforced me as a car guy, and not just a Ford corporate guy.

I've been a car guy pretty much my whole life and I've been lucky to have been involved with racing in some form for a long time now. Over my car guy time, I've been a Honda Guy, a Ford Guy, a team owner, a driver, a marketer, and a designer. Each step got me to where I am today.

I started racing Hondas when there were no Honda parts to speak of. Oscar Jackson of Jackson Racing, King Motorsports from Wisconsin, and Lightspeed from Florida were pretty much the only sources for parts.

A few years later came the Integra GS-R with a motor that could easily be swapped into a 90s Civic or CRX. The Honda tuning culture exploded. Civics and CRXs were cheap and Integras kept getting crashed, so there were lots of B18 motors. B18s could handle a ton of boost, so the Honda drag racing scene grew quickly.

Over time, I learned more and more about Hondas and the engineering behind them. I became an advocate for all of my friends and family, even converting my Mopar-muscle-car-loving, road-racing teammate from a Dodge to a Honda. I was the Honda guy in our paddock and even though I didn't intend to be, I branded myself as the Honda guy.

This continued during my career at Ford, where I became a performance guy. When in public, representing Ford either as Mustang Brand Manager or as the Performance and Enthusiast Marketing Manager, I was branding myself into those roles. I became, through these two roles, a Ford guy. While still a Honda guy at heart, I embraced the passion of the Ford enthusiasts and dug into what makes the Mustang brand so compelling that people spend weeks of their lives at car shows sitting in lawn chairs showing off their rare Mustangs.

I was still champion of my own brand, but I brought background and perspective to my public engagements. When representing Fiesta, for example, I would be as honest about the car's awesomeness as I was about it being an entry-level car and not on par with more expensive models. Adding perspective to the discussions helped me retain my car guy-ness. As I transitioned into Ford Performance, I got to spread my wings and embrace the performance side of things. It was a long way from working on Fusion Hybrid and Edge for China. I embraced my brand as a car guy's car guy. I fought for the performance customer as we sought to give them the best car at the best price with the most amazing performance that Ford Performance could offer.

As I transitioned out of Ford and am now on my own as a team owner, driver, storyteller, and author, I've found freedom to embrace all those aspects of my personal brand. The people who knew me as the Mustang Guy still know me as that. The people who knew me as a Honda guy still know me as that. The racers who I've competed with over the years know a different version.

All of those personal brands have one thing in common and that's me—my personality, my curiosity, my passion, my sense of right and wrong, my perseverance, and my drive. As I begin yet another chapter of this amazingly fun life, I get to bring this brand history with me and bring forward the elements that work and downplay those that don't. The most fun bit of all is that as I share my knowledge on branding, I'm always learning and finding more to share.

A LASTING IMPRESSION

We, as club racers, haven't turned pro yet, but we can still present ourselves, our teams, and, most importantly, our cars as professional. So how do we alter the perception of our friends and family from club racer and hobbyist to aspiring pro? It's actually easier than it sounds.

I recommend starting simple. How would you want someone to describe you and your racing program? Winning, strong, quick, fast, humble? Find the right adjective to describe your style and strengthen it. Brand yourself.

Sounds a little pretentious but, the thing is, you've already branded yourself with every interaction on track and off. Your personal brand is the sum of people's opinions about you and the impression you leave them with. It's your choice how you interact with each fan, official, or partner.

Personal branding is about more than just your personality, though. There are several key steps to creating and building a personal brand. Think of the phrase, "They wore their trademark XYZ," or "…with their trademark XYZ." When you think of F1 driver Daniel Ricciardo, you instantly think of that infectious smile. When you think of John Force, you think of that boundless energy.

What is your trademark going to be? Think about how you present yourself on track. What are your habits? Do you always wear the same kind of shirt, the same hat, or the same sunglasses? If so, then each of those things is part of your personal brand. Your personal brand is made up of uniqueness combined with consistency. You have this great laugh, great smile, you're always serious, you're quiet, you're loud, you're a partier, or not. Your personality is a key driver of your personal brand.

As a club racer, how do you set yourself apart from everyone else while still being you? The best part about this is that you keep doing what you do. Just be more consistent with it. If you like wearing t-shirts to the track, then pick two or three and wear the same ones. Or, wear ones with the same theme each time you're at the track. Remember the architect rule of threes—apply it here.

Think about the image you present to the world at the racetrack. We'll talk a little more about this in the social media chapter, but the image you present in person and in social media should be fairly close to each other. Each of us is going to approach personal branding a little differently. If you consistently act one way, consistently present yourself in a way, you become more memorable and your personal brand becomes a shorthand for people when they think of you.

SHOW YOUR FACE

One key to becoming more recognized is to be visible. This applies to online and social media more than anything. When you start out in club racing, people don't know who you are or what you look like. It is important for you to be the face of your personal brand.

This is just what it sounds like. Make your face well-known. Be in your pictures—selfies are awesome. Have others get snaps and videos of you at the track, too. Let people hear your voice. Your personal brand is going to be infused with your personality, but it needs you to drive it forward. You need to be the face of your brand.

The more you can get your face and voice out there, the more people will connect your personal brand with your face and voice. This will reinforce your personal brand personality and brand voice. Being consistent and being visible are the two most important parts of building your personal brand.

And it's totally ok to be consistent with your inconsistency. Are you curious and all over the place? Then embrace it. But, be consistently all over the place, be visible, and, most of all, be yourself. Do this and you can take your personal brand anywhere you want to. It's your You be You. So run with it!

HARDEST-WORKING PEOPLE AT THE TRACK

Your team has personality and personal brands as well. Think of any of the car-building shows you've watched over the past several years. They all have personalities. From the owners to the techs, they all add to the soul of the show.

Your team is the same. Highlight them, show their faces, put them on camera, and build the presence of your club team. They will become a group of people others will want to get to know. By showing the faces of your team, you make your team more real and you breathe personality into your brand beyond that of the drivers. We all know who does all the hard work around race cars and the team rarely gets the recognition they deserve.

One cool way to do this is through day-in-the-life pictures or video of your crew doing what they do—working on cars, hanging out, having fun, being deep in conversation.

CURB APPEAL

For most of us club racers, we're a smaller operation. This doesn't mean our paddock space can't have presence. It goes back to what you want others to think of you and your setup. Sure, we don't have a $500k toter home setup, but we do have our car, our space, our tow vehicle and trailer, our race cars, and our pop-up tent.

We spent the time on the branding, now let's show it off a bit and bring it all together. The team looks awesome, the race car looks awesome, now our home away from home needs to get dressed up a bit.

Where do we start to create that branded experience? Take a look at your paddock setup and think about what you would like to change, not just from a branded point of view, but from a useability point of view. Do you need more workspace, more light, whatever? Fix those first and get yourself to a point where you feel comfortable spending money on shiny stuff for your paddock spot. Make sure you've solved as many of the paddock issues as you reasonably can before spending time and energy on branding. Those can be a distraction if you aren't ready.

Once you're ready, take a step back and look at your setup and see it as a stranger would. Remember when you did that paddock walk? Think of it now as a research project for how you want your paddock space to look. What makes the largest impact to you? What are the branded elements that resonate with you? Would you know that Racer X was set up here? No? How do we change that?

The key to building a branded paddock space is to do it in stages and not to take big swings. Stay true to your brand and your team colors when buying things for the paddock if you can. If your team colors are orange and black and you need a table for your driver helmets and the choices are gray or black, get black. Another way to brand your space is to place a sticker with your logo on your gear. It's a simple but effective way to extend your brand without spending much.

Purchase things with a long life in your team colors so that they will fit in for years to come. If you need a doormat for the trailer, get one that is in keeping with the team brand or team colors. It doesn't have to be branded, it just needs to fit in.

When you buy mundane things like tables, chairs, and extension cords, if you can't get things in your team colors, go for consistency. The things you buy for your paddock space don't have to be fancy, just consistent. Part of branding your paddock space is to build an environment that looks planned and not accumulated. Try to get the same kinds of chairs, the same kinds of tables. You should know it's your space when you walk in and not a mishmash of whatever was available at the time.

EYES UP

Now we're going to get into things that do cost money. As a club racer, it seems weird to spend money on things that don't make the car go faster on track. As you look around your paddock space and take a step back, you'll see the most visible thing in your paddock space from a distance is your awning or your popup.

It's quite expensive to brand a popup, often costing $500 or more for a custom top for a 10 x 10 and around $1,500 or more for a 10 x 20. If you are going to get a popup and you don't want to spring for your logo on it, choose a top that is in one of your team colors.

Focus on your core color or colors. You want the popup to complement the team palette. If you can swing branding your popup, make sure you do it on all four sides and the valances as well. Use your brand guidelines to help guide the designers at the popup or awning company to create a design that is in line with your brand, your logo, and your team colors.

A simpler and less expensive way to get yourself noticed is to put up a flag with your logo on it. Collapsible flagpoles are relatively inexpensive and a custom flag is usually under $150. A custom flag takes a few weeks to get made. With one, you get your logo and brand high in the air above a sea of color. The flag becomes an easy landmark and complements any paddock space. You can also do banners and sail-type flags, but these tend to be lower to the ground and have a little less impact on the overall experience from a distance.

One tip on flags: when you do choose to order, try to get three at a time. You usually get a quantity discount and often flags fade over time. This way, you'll have one ready to go when the first one fades.

Why the third flag? Well, it's great to have one at the shop or to hang in the trailer. Another fun thing to do is to fly your race team flag at your house when you are competing.

LIGHTING AND POST-RACE AMENITIES

Your paddock space often stays alive late into the night. How you light your paddock space says a lot about how it is organized and set up. First and foremost, after the sun has set you'll need to be able to see well to work on the race car. The current LED lights for awnings and popups have a huge impact. When in doubt about lighting for your paddock space, get more. More is almost always better in this case. We laugh about turning night into day when we turn the lights on.

Your paddock space should feel like an extension of the race shop—well-lit and comfortable to work and play in. After hours, if things are going well, you may want to relax and put your feet up for a beer with the team and bench race until late at night. A well-lit, comfortable paddock space is key to keeping your crew happy.

Think about amenities for your crew and drivers and use lighting to create separate spaces in your area for working on cars and for hanging out and eating or drinking. Think of this as you would your deck at home. Lots of home improvement deck-building shows can give you inspiration. This separation of spaces is another element of your overall paddock space branding. It speaks to your brand and is a key element of the functionality of your paddock space.

FEED YOUR CREW

So, you've made your paddock space awesome, now you need to set up your hospitality space. Here is another place where you can get super creative to save money. If you always cook at the track and put the food out on a table for all to walk through buffet-style, then invest in a branded table cover for the food table. It doesn't have to be super fancy, but it speaks to your brand. Table covers are typically pretty reasonable.

You can go super overboard with amenities and branding here. You be You, but try to be restrained a bit. While it might be fun to get branded plastic cups and plastic plates, you don't want your logo thrown in the garbage. Instead, find cups and plates that are in your team colors. Do a sleeve of one team color and one of the other. Choose plates the same way. These little things tie the branded experience together. Maybe the cooler is in one of the team colors or has a team sticker on it.

The point here is that you make a conscious choice to be consistent to tie your branded theme together.

TOW VEHICLE AND TRAILER

Branding the tow vehicle and trailer can become super expensive if you wrap the whole thing. Maybe we can brand smarter and less expensively. How about adding just your logo to both tow vehicle and trailer? Now add in your race number, your partner logos, and just one of the team colors as an accent to save on vinyl costs.

Be creative here and you'll add a little reasonably-priced branded goodness. The tow vehicle and trailer are visible branded tools both when in transport and while sitting still at the track. They are a part of the overall branded experience, but are background items. Think of them as such. The real branding power in your paddock space comes from the car, the awning, the flags, the space, and the amenities. Pay attention to the branding on your trailer and see where the awning or popup exposes the side of the trailer as backdrop. Can you use this space on the side of the trailer to serve as a branded backdrop when you have the awning up or the popup next to it?

Create a branded backdrop that is tailored to the space you are using. Some awnings are large and come off the top of the trailer, leaving tons of room for inside branding. Some use a 10 x 10 popup that has less space for branding on the trailer beside it.

Your truck and trailer branding is an opportunity to extend your brand and enhance the space in which you interact with fans, followers, friends, and family.

Your paddock space is an extension of the branded experience you provide to your team. Each chance you have to bring your brand or team colors forward and build on that environment helps tie things together and strengthens the branded experience.

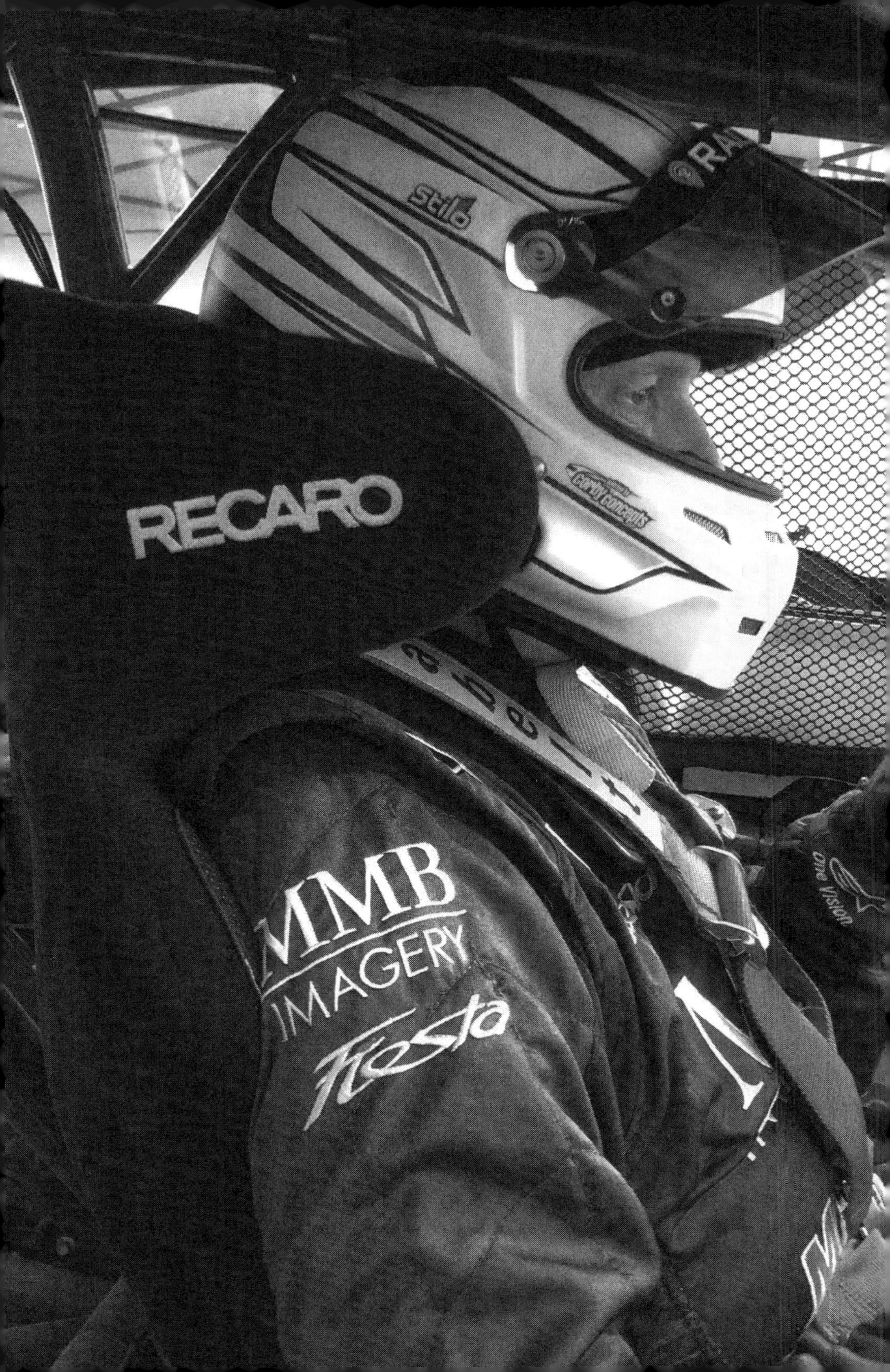
stilo
RECARO
MMB
IMAGERY
Fiesta

12

BUILDING YOUR BRANDED GEAR STORE

It's 2010. My wife and I are visiting friends in Australia.

We walked into a pro rugby fan shop and at the front is the New Zealand section. There was a Ford logo looking right at me. And another, and another. Ford sponsored the New Zealand rugby league and the Ford logo was on all the team jerseys. I brought a few home.

Later, we visited Bathurst. Because, well, you kind of have to if you're in Sydney. It's only a few hours to the west. We drove the track; amazing place! The view from the top of the mountain is awesome. I had no idea how many houses were along ConRod Straight. It's driveway after driveway on the left.

We stopped at the museum near the track and I picked up some track souvenirs. Later on, when we were back in Sydney, we found a small motorsports shop tucked away in a local mall. At first, I was looking for a cool Falcon diecast to bring back to work. I was fascinated with the FPR logo. The Falcon and Commodore were forbidden fruit in the US, so it was cool to experience them first hand.

Then, I started looking through the team gear. Holy Moly! I thought about how well they were being marketed. There were about a dozen shirt options and just about every branded item you can think of with driver and team sponsor logos. In Australia, Super V8s are just like our NASCAR. They get marketing and they do it very well.

We, as FWR, weren't ready for a team store just yet; that was in the future. But I absorbed what I saw and made mental notes of what I liked and didn't. The experience planted a seed of knowledge. I noted they separated their merchandise into supporter and team gear.

Supporter gear was a little simpler and less expensive and team gear was the opposite—very expensive and quite close to the real gear the team wore. It was very official looking. Of course, I went for the team gear as I wanted one for myself, but I also got some supporter gear.

As we grew the FWR brand in 2016, I kept thinking back to the Aussie V8 merchandise in that little shop. I was super excited to open up our first online store. I'd done the branding and promotion and I felt like the FWR shop was ready to open. Thing was, our logo wasn't that interesting, and we didn't really have a hook.

I loved our new logo and I had put a lot of time into it, but it was mostly family who purchased our items. I was so excited to build out this amazing presence and then as sales fell flat, I tried different promotions, different sales tactics, discounts, you name it. After a while, I realized that the draw just wasn't there. There was a reason this wasn't working and I was going to find it.

Around this time, a good friend told me that he supported me, but he wasn't going to wear my name on his shirt. Ever. "Love ya, man, but not doing it. Not going to wear your name on my chest."

I love it when people are super clear! Right then I realized the problem. My team name and team name brand wasn't going to get it done in the merch world.

"You need a logo, like Gas Monkey Garage or Orange County Choppers. Something cool that people will want to wear," he said.

Fast forward a few years. I learned team branding lessons and I built the

Ollie Rocket Racing store with Will's octopus merch. The logo and the story behind the brand resonated; people want to help kids succeed in sports. Eventually supporters started to buy Ollie Rocket Racing merchandise—stickers, shirts, hoodies, you name it. We make it clear that all the proceeds go towards funding Will's karting.

Our merchandise store idea started some 14,000 miles away in an obscure shop in Sydney, Australia. Team gear and supporter gear isn't a new thing by any means, but as I look at building mainstream draw beyond friends and family, I realize that it's another lever we have as marketers to build our brand.

DO YOU HAVE THE TIME?

A merchandise store is a great way to supplement your racing budget once you get it up and running. Let's take a look at what it takes to make a merch store successful. Your store may be at the track every weekend, it might be an online store, or it could be a combination.

Merch stores can be a pain in the butt, but they can also be awesome. If you have the time to build and manage a team store, it can extend your team brand. Or, they can become a real job on top of your real job.

Before you begin your store, find others in your series who are doing it. Reach out to the owners and ask them how much time they commit to it, how they set it up, and who they sell to. Be fearless here. Some team store owners will see you as a threat and won't help much, while others will welcome you. Heck, you might find someone willing to be an additional outlet for your merch, you never know.

What you want to know is initial setup time and store management time. If you will be fulfilling the orders, you need to make sure that you have a foolproof way of getting notified when someone buys your merch. There are several online tools to help you here. That way, you can get it boxed up and sent on time. Once you have asked a few people about their store, you'll get a general idea of what it takes to do it successfully.

One thing to consider before you open a team store is taxes. Typically, you will be required to collect sales tax for items you sell in your state. This involves applying for a sales tax collection license. It's called something different in each state. Do a search for sales tax licenses in your state to learn more.

Understand the tax implications of selling something to someone out of state as well. There are online resources available to help you. Make sure you apply for and receive your license from your home state before opening your store. Missing this and correcting this later can make for an expensive tax bill.

YOUR BRAND IN A BAR FIGHT

Let's tackle team gear first before we get into setting up your merch store. Simpler is better here, especially if you have limited funds. You aren't going to change your logo anytime soon, so let's start there. You can create one shirt design for the whole team. This will help you build a branded presence quickly.

My recommendation is to build gear that will last season over season. Partners change, but your logo and team colors will not. The fun thing about this is that you can really focus on your team branding. Your team gear should consist of your main brand color and accent colors. Your team shirts should have your logo on the front and your team name on the back or vice versa. You decide which look you like the best. Make your team gear the best representation of your brand.

If you decide to create more elaborate team gear or different categories of team gear, there are some guidelines that will help you. Team gear should highlight your key partners and your team logo. Split your team gear in three categories: crew, drivers, and owners. The theme of your team gear should be the same, just add in subtle differences for each category.

The crew gear should be durable and in a color or design that helps hide the inevitable stains from working on cars. Dye-sublimated or screen-printed work shirts, t-shirts or Dri-fits work best here. Be kind to your crew and get them shirts that breathe.

Your driver gear should be a level up from your team gear. If your team gear is a t-shirt or work shirt, then your driver gear should be a Dri-fit polo.

Owner gear is another level up from driver gear, so think button-down or dress shirt with the team logo and key partners embroidered on them. Owner gear's main purpose is to make owners easy for partners to identify in the sea of team gear.

Out-to-dinner team gear consists of Dri-fit polos or button downs with just the team logo on the left chest and the team name across the upper back. These are used for going out to dinner or for being on camera away from the track. At least once a weekend, we go out to dinner as a team. This is where we are all together as one big family.

Now we're ready for fan gear. You want it to be obvious who is with the team and who is a fan. Team gear provides a sense of officialness that fan gear does not. You don't want someone who looks like your crew to be a part of a bar fight.

As club racers, we'll want to have fan gear that is instantly recognizable and different from team gear. Fan gear is less detailed and less specific than team gear. It doesn't mean fan gear is less awesome, it needs to be awesome, it's just not as specific as team gear. If team gear is two colors, then fan gear will be one. If team gear is embroidered, then fan gear is printed.

HOW TO SET UP A STORE

When you're experimenting with fan gear those first few months, start small. Be simple and listen to your customers. Don't be afraid to contact them and ask them what they would like to purchase. You'll be surprised by the responses. People love to help guide store selection.

Choosing stickers is next. By experimenting small, you limit your initial risk. Stickers are a low-investment item and carry a lot of margin. Start small with lots of 100–250 stickers of various designs until you see what sells. It may cost more per piece, but you're looking for a winner. You can order larger amounts later.

Typically, we go with a logo sticker in two different colors and a sticker of a spotter's guide drawing of the car. There are other options: the team name, the driver name, the car number with the team name. Take a look at your series and see what others are doing for merch in this category. Start small and learn. You can also look for some cool label sheets and print them yourself. Check out your local craft store for options.

For t-shirts, go with things people know. For shirts, this is typically a small logo or lettering on the upper-left chest and a larger design on the back. Spend the time to make an amazing design. A well-designed shirt costs as much as a poorly designed one.

Once you get the hang of it, start expanding your offerings—two colors of long-sleeve shirts and two colors of short-sleeve shirts for youth, men, and women. Already you have 12 options for shirts, and we haven't talked sizes yet.

It grows quickly! Printing partner logos and your team name in one color can be cost effective here.

You can choose Dri-fit, soft-touch cottons, or regular shirts. Take a look at what others are wearing at your events. Recently, kids seem to be moving more towards Dri-fit clothing, so you may want to make sure you have a Dri-fit option for them.

Now, sweatshirts, hoodies, or ¼ zips. Choose two of these in two colors for youth, men, and women. 12 more options for the store. The time we spent on brand guidelines will make picking the right logo for the colors pretty easy.

Baseball caps come in a million different variations, but the three main versions are the mesh-backed trucker, individually sized flex-fit, or regular where they have a Velcro, snap, or buckle strap for sizing. Take your time and find ones that fit your brand.

Once you have the basics covered, you can expand into other items like keychains, umbrellas, koozies, or tumblers. There are a ton of choices out there. Take the time to brand the store, then fill in the merchandise. It is a pain to do the other way around.

Ask lots of questions of friends and family—see what they want and what they like. Use this to guide you as you expand your store.

TO HOLD INVENTORY OR NOT

At first, you aren't going to have a handle on what sells. It can be intimidating to order merchandise that has potential to sit on the shelf. Using a print-on-demand company is a good way to start. You will pay a little more because they are holding the inventory. As your store grows and thrives, you can wean yourself off print-on-demand.

Approach your local print shops and ask them to host your store and fulfill the orders. This is often more cost effective than using the big online stores. Local stores can batch print to fill up dead time on their presses.

As you grow your store, you'll be able to order ahead of time to meet demand. This is more cost-efficient, but it does mean you're investing in and managing inventory. I write this while looking at a whole bunch of one particular item that's sitting on my desk looking for a home....

If you have a physical merch trailer at the track, keep the initial offerings simple and listen to what your customers are asking you for. Over time, you'll find your particular market.

WEBSITE OR SOCIAL

Okay, we know what we want to sell, now where are we going to sell it? For most of us, this will be online. There are two main avenues for this: social media or on your website. Both take about the same amount of effort to set up and both have similar selling fees. Your real decision is about platform. If you put your energy into social media, then that's probably a good place to put your store. If you drive people to your website, then head in that direction.

Let's take a look at a website store first.

With a website store, you control the way gear is presented. You sort out the merch into categories more easily on a website than on a social media sales site. Hosting and sales fees are pretty similar to social media options. I like a website store primarily for the seamless, branded experience I can create.

You can also use social media to drive traffic to your website store. There's really no wrong way here.

How about a social media store?

A social media store serves as an advertising platform and a selling platform. The targeting and demographics data can help grow your reach. As research, the next time you see a sale link on Facebook or Instagram, click and see where it takes you.

You'll likely find about 50/50 direct to site and direct to social. There are several services designed to help you get a social media store set up. There are also several tutorials on setting up a social media shop. Try them out to see what works best for you. For both options, you can choose to do print-on-demand, batch print, or hold inventory.

BUSINESS SCHOOL

Before you get too far down this road, get a handle on how base costs work. For example, color t-shirts are typically more expensive than white or gray. Black is typically the most expensive because of the extra dye needed. Cotton, soft-touch cotton, and Dri-fit also have higher costs with Dri-fit typically being the most expensive.

Another item that drives print cost is multiple colors. A garment is placed onto a press and a screen with the graphic is placed on top of the garment. Then, ink is poured onto the screen and smoothed out across the garment. This process is repeated for each color on the garment. The more colors you have, the more time it takes.

Each unique location also adds time and cost. This is the same for printing and embroidery—the more locations, the more expensive. It's easy to create an awesome shirt with lots of locations and colors that has $30 in production costs alone!

Embroidery is more expensive than screen printing. The more intricate your logo, the more threads you need and the more expensive the embroidery. The same goes for size: larger is more expensive.

Once you have the costs, add a certain percentage as your profit. This is called cost-plus pricing. You may find that the market is willing to pay a lot more than your cost-plus for a specific item. Price accordingly. Sometimes this works the other way. In the real world, your customers decide what items are worth and buy them or don't.

I'm looking at that set of items I mentioned before and wondering why in the world I thought these keychains would sell for $25. I hadn't checked the market well enough. They're awesome and I love them, but there just isn't a market for $25 keychains.

Knowing your price point helps you prioritize the locations you want printed. Ultimately, you want your effort to pay off in the long run. Do your homework and know your costs. You will find that this baseline, more than anything, will help you make your merchandise decisions.

MAKE YOUR STORE MAKE SENSE

Your store needs to make financial sense. How do you make sure it is working for you? You track all of your costs. Sounds simple, but you can get deep into a rabbit hole here. Just as you budget for your race team, you need to budget for your store. There are free online budget spreadsheets that can help you with this. Break your costs into three main categories: maintenance, shipping, and material costs.

In the maintenance category, include online fees and general costs related to hosting the store. If your store is physical, include transportation costs here.

For shipping, include packing materials, boxes, and postage. This is included if you use a print-on-demand service, but if you're doing it yourself, keep track. You can treat it like maintenance or include it in every order. Some customers like the carrot of free shipping. If you offer free shipping, make sure you understand the average costs and build it into the price of your items.

Material costs should include design and production costs as well as material. For production costs, you will need to get quotes from your suppliers or print-on-demand company for each item you sell. You may have a high-priced item that makes little margin and a low-priced one that crushes it. Knowing the real costs on your merch will help you run a profitable store.

ON TOUR

For all this talk of consistency and cost savings, I still love doing season-specific gear. We mostly do this for our core supporters as it is expensive to produce. If you want to do this, I recommend two approaches. First, you can do higher-priced garments like ¼ zips and Dri-fit polos. Higher-priced garments typically have more ability to absorb cost. Mark these items for print-on-demand by your local shop. Second, unique, season-specific stickers are a low-investment item and each design can be unique. As long as you keep the year off them, you can sell them at normal prices for as long as you want.

One fun exception to this is a season tour shirt. Think concert tour. People *love* these shirts! Put your logo on the front of the shirt—normally over the left chest—and underneath your logo, put something like "2022 Season". Then, on the back, put your logo at the top with "2022 Season" again, this time larger.

Underneath, list each track name, location, and date on the back. Something like this:

Sebring International Raceway
Sebring, Florida | January 27-29

Circuit of the Americas
Austin, Texas | February 9-11

Road Atlanta
Braselton, Georgia | May 12-14

Road America
Elkhart Lake, Wisconsin | June 4-6

Watkins Glen International
Watkins Glen, New York | July 12-14

It should read like stops on a concert tour. You can even label it as your 2022 US Tour. These are typically pretty popular items. Have fun with this.

WB

Over the past several years, we created season-specific gear as a thank you for our financial supporters. We also create gear that's reserved exclusively for our Team FWR members.

For Ollie Rocket, we've taken this a step further and introduced WB, or Will's Buddies. This gear is offered exclusively to Will's friends in school and karting. Only Will's friends are able to buy WB gear.

Will created his own WB logo to do this. It is typically a limited selection of merchandise in the store, but with a WB logo added. It's a way to reward Will's friends and build a club of fans early on. Simple things like this can make for a unique selection of items.

TRY, FAIL, AND ADJUST

Just as we track costs, we need to track sales. If we thought the market would bear $20 for our shirt and they aren't moving, we need to change price. You may find that you sell out a different item instantly. Awesome! There's an opportunity to increase the price a little for the next batch. Don't worry about lost profit. Make it on the next one.

Look at your sales, make adjustments, and move on. Try, fail, and adjust. On your spreadsheet, put notes for price and method changes so you can see what works. It's much easier to do when you're making the change rather than trying to remember later.

You're most of the way through the season and you're looking at your inventory. There's a pile of shirts, hats, and stickers. Time for an end-of-season sale! Put in a site-wide discount and move the merch before the end of the year. Be sure to do this before your last race of the year. Once the season is over, it takes quite a bit more work to generate energy around your club racing brand. Get your cash out of the merchandise sitting in front of you.

If you know you're changing partners and you have a ton of logoed items, get them moving. The only exception is if you want to hold them for a year or two and put them up later as retro items. This can work for some people. If your brand is well established and it is making a big change, then hang onto a few. If not, it's best to clear out your inventory, learn what sold, and what did not.

Try, fail, adjust. This should be your store motto: learn with every failure and every success.

PART III

BUILD YOUR RACING BRAND ONLINE

13

GENERATING CONTENT

It's the 1994 season. Let's revisit the accident from Brainerd. I didn't know it at the time, but one of my friends, Pat Doyle, was shooting pictures at that corner. He captured a series of images of the car as it went end over end and came back down. The last image in the series is of the car sitting on its side and me walking towards the ambulance.

This was my first real sense of the importance of photographers at the track and the importance of generating content. Photographers capture moments that we never can. We are there in the car, we have our in-car and on-car video, but we rarely get footage or images from outside the car when we first start.

I still have those pictures Pat shot all these years later. I marvel at how high off the ground the car was at one point as it rotated around the center of mass at the engine. I don't have any pictures of it hiking up the inside rear wheel, hopping a curb, or coming out of a corner. The pictures I have are of it mid-accident and mid-air. They are the first and only real pictures I have of that race car.

Now, at each event we attend, I find the local photographers and ask for pictures of my car on track and my team in the paddock. Looking back, I wish I had done the same with the Civic and CRX from years ago.

Fast forward to 2018, and we're at Road America for the June Sprints. I followed Kent Carter in his Honda Fit into turn five as we swept past Tommy Coury in his Mazda2. We were catching James Wilson in his Mazda2.

As we headed up to six, Kent missed a shift. I ran into the back of Kent and Tommy careened off me and into James. James pounded into the wall under the bridge. His car came off the wall and back into my car. We both spun to a long, noisy stop at the top of the hill.

The thousand or so people at the outside of turn six did the golf clap when I got out of the car. I waved to signal that I was ok. My car was heavily damaged, but repairable. We'd be back on track for the next event in two weeks at GingerMan.

There was a ton of video from the various cars, and everyone involved posted lots of pictures. All trying to figure out exactly what had happened in the complicated accident. All of that content generated engagement.

We made it to GingerMan and I was running strong in the Saturday race. As I turned into the quick right-hander leading onto the front straight, I heard a "PING" noise. The left front wheel went sailing off into the distance.

Cars on three wheels stop pretty fast when they go into a gravel trap. We'd had a hub failure. We shared the series of pictures of the car digging into the gravel on three wheels, the remains of the failed hub, the guys working on the car late into the night, and our thoughts on the past two weeks.

Throughout the entire episode, we were getting messages of support. We started to understand how much our followers were engaged in our adventures and our content. Their support helped us turned a negative into a positive, especially after our accident at Road America.

FOCUS...FOCUS...

Most content you can and should create yourself. With a little practice, you'll find you can take great pictures during the race weekend. Here are some quick tips on creating amazing imagery.

Composition—Our eyes are excellent at blurring out backgrounds. Cameras are not. Pictures with a short depth of field are usually so compelling because they look like what we see. Pay attention to your background first. Make sure that your subject is not overwhelmed by a noisy background.

Focus—Make sure you focus on your subject before you take the picture.

Cropping—Ad research in the 40s uncovered the imagery rule of two. People's eyes typically scan an image in a path resembling the number "2". They start at the upper left, cross over to the right, then they go diagonally across to the lower left before finishing in the lower right. If you want to catch someone's eye quickly, upper left it is. If you want to hide something, put it in the lower right.

Grids—Most software will give you gridlines in thirds. Try to put the subject's eye or face on the intersection of any of these grid lines. We connect with our subject's eyes and faces. It's a simple way to make strong photographs.

Light—Place the sunlight at an angle onto the front of your subject. Make sure your shadow isn't in the picture, unless that's what you're highlighting. Some phones are great at creating fill-in light and some are not, so you may need to use your flash, even in daylight.

CREDIT WHERE CREDIT IS DUE

Here are some tips for working with pro photographers.

One of the easiest ways to find pro photographers is to reach out to your competitors. Ask who they've been using and approach that photographer to see if they can add you. Connect at least a week or two ahead of the event.

If you haven't connected with a photographer before the event, you can find them at the track. If you see anyone in a media vest, ask them. They'll point you in the right direction. If your series has a PR manager, see who they're using for the weekend.

Once you're connected with a photographer, ask for four things: content, pricing, rights, and timing.

Content—Ask for on-track, paddock, and day-in-the-life shots. We ask our photographers to shoot in our paddock at some point during the weekend. Make sure your crew members are in branded gear and project the brand image you have crafted for your team. If you're all about having fun as a team, make sure they're smiling and goofing around after the race. If you're a serious brand, focus on the work. One other thing: ask for a few images of the people who make a race weekend possible—marshals, grid workers, corner workers, and stewards. Give back a little. Give these images to the people who make race weekends possible. Say thank you in person and on social media. It's the right thing to do and it also increases reach and engagement.

Pricing—Make sure you pay for quantity and variety. Our typical, all-rights agreement with our photographer friends is between $80 and $150 per weekend for about 100-150 images. Some tracks and photographers can cost more. If we've hired the photographer to shoot our team exclusively, we expect to spend $400-500.

Rights—Some photographers give personal rights and commercial rights for different fees; some give all-rights usage regardless. Since your intent is to use the imagery to promote your racing, ask for all-rights including commercial. It can get complicated, so secure all the rights when you can. Every photographer likes to have their work credited. When you share an image you've purchased from a photographer, please give them credit. It can be a tag on social media or a flowery thank you. Either way, give them credit for the work they do.

Timing—You can get images same day if you ask up front. I like to have two or three each day that I can add to our race recap posts. If you ask and they deliver, get them posted. You know how you'd feel if the roles were reversed. Normally, the rest of the race weekend images are available about a week after the event.

SHARE CONTENT WITH PARTNERS

Your partners want to see you and they want on-track images and videos. If you've gotten the commercial rights to the content, you can share it with your partners for their advertising purposes. Pro images and video are often too large to email, so use a file sharing service.

Once a year, print an image, sign it with a thank you note, and put it in the mail to your partners. You'll be glad you did. Think about your office and the things you keep there. Now think about your marketing partner who doesn't get to go to the races. A quick thank you note goes a long, long way.

QUALIFY, RACE, WIN, CELEBRATE

Before the weekend starts, we have an idea how our story is going to unfold. We plan to prep the car, load up the car, transport the car, arrive, set up our paddock space, get ready for the first session, qualify, race, win, celebrate, tear down the paddock space, load up the car, transport it home, unload it into the shop, and begin prepping it for the next event.

Whew!…wait. Go back. Read that again. Look at the content opportunities! Each of these brings you and your brand closer to your audience. It's easy to miss the best moments.

Sharing content after the event has the feel of a tape-delayed broadcast. "Here is what we are doing right now" is much more powerful than "Here's what we did this weekend." How do you avoid tape-delayed posts?

Have a content plan. A content plan will help you cover off weeks, race weekends, and travel to and from the track. Write out your content plan, even if it's just bullets. Build a framework ahead of time. Put it up on the wall of the trailer. Add, delete, and check them off the list.

Plan on five posts from the time you get to the track until the time you leave. Take pictures from multiple angles during setup. Think of these as backups so while you're packing up, you already have the images, you didn't miss anything. Add some text and drop a post.

If you race at the same track each weekend, travel between a limited number of tracks, or are somewhere different each weekend, you will approach your content plan differently.

Let's start with competing in the same few places week after week. The tracks and backgrounds stay the same, so focus your content plan around your team. Turn the lens to the crew and the drivers. Create content stories about your team.

What about arriving, racing, and going home the same day? A plan is essential in this case. Try pre-populating some written content like, "Heading out for qualifying," or, "We're on at 430." This will take some of the pressure off. Add a quick image and hit send when you have a spare moment.

If you always paddock in the same spot, build a story about your home away from home. It can be a new mascot brought by someone's kids, better beer, or new chairs in the paddock. Look for on-brand content that fits.

If you travel to several different tracks, build variety into your content for the weekend. Are there great racing restaurants or bars close by where you make a point to go to for dinner or drinks? Take a group picture and share your experience.

General content ideas:

Arrival day:

- We got here safe and sound
- Race cars are tucked in
- Sunset pictures
- My office for tomorrow

Qualifying day:

- We head out at XYZ time—follow along here
- Competitors and the conditions
- Results and the story of the session

Race day:

- Ready to start
- Race starts at XYZ time—follow along here
- Ready to go
- Race results

Post-race content ideas:

- Video of you talking about the race

- Fixing the car at the shop
- Impressions of the race, the track, and your performance
- Your place in the championship
- Closeups of partner's products on the race cars

#TBT

Throwback Thursday has been around at least since a 2011 HotWheels post on Instagram. #TBTs help create a backstory for your brand. They are a look back at your world. They can also increase your audience as #TBT is followed by millions of people.

Use an old image—pre-internet if you can. It can even be a picture of a photograph. It can be faded, slightly blurry, or black and white.

If you're going racing this weekend, find an old image of the track you're headed to. This can be interesting if track configurations, signage, or buildings have changed significantly. Or, share a picture of friends and family. Maybe an accident picture or victory circle. It doesn't have to be about racing either. It could be you with 80s hair or 90s flannel, you at graduation, whatever. Pick your story, find your image, and run with it.

Short and sweet often wins at #TBT. Example: #TBT to that time I was hanging upside down in my belts at Blackhawk Farms.

Embrace your history, even when it's seriously embarrassing. It's part of what makes this fun. It puts a little more soul in your brand. You can make a dozen #TBT posts in one session and then schedule them to be posted every week at a specific time. People can do #TBT pretty much any day using the general On This Day. You'll be surprised at how quickly you get into the groove.

SHOULD YOU SHARE CONTENT FROM OTHERS?

Think about how it fits with your brand. Stay on brand with content shares and likes to put more depth in your brand. Pick the content you share carefully, and you can use it to extend your brand, give your brand a little more soul.

One caveat. Be careful with politics. Many people follow our sport as an escape from everyday noise and drama. When your sport or your team gets into politics, be prepared to lose touch with some of your audience. Use caution here. Do what's best for you and your brand—you be you.

VIDEO KILLED THE RADIO STAR

Video is a super-effective way to get a ton of reach. We club racers often have tons of video, but very little is shot from outside the car. This is where live video can come to the rescue. You will engage your audience with behind-the-scenes content.

Nobody likes the sound of their own voice. I'm on the Performance Motorsports Network at every race, and I still cringe when I hear my voice on the PA. Don't worry about being self-conscious. Practice by yourself at first. It doesn't matter what you talk about. You're just trying to see what works.

Once you get comfortable behind the camera, try a short welcome video. You are the narrator and the camera should be facing you, so you will have your back to the things you are showing your fans.

Lots of us want to walk when we talk on camera. You want to show your race car, your paddock spot, or maybe inside the hauler, but know where you're going beforehand. Have a plan. Try it like this: I'm going to start here and then I'm going to walk over here by the driver's side of the race car and then I'm going to walk out from under the awning.

Match the pace of your video to the pace of your background. Frame your shots and control your background to eliminate distraction. This is why many selfie videos are shot in a car—there are no outside distractions. Once you get good at managing backgrounds, you can play with tension between background and foreground; crazy chaos behind you and you're just calmly talking away.

Oh, one more thing. Capture your video in landscape format. It's far easier for your fans to watch you in landscape than in portrait mode.

A DASH OF VOICE-OVER, A SMIDGE OF SLO-MO

If video production is not for you, the next section on hiring a videographer is going to be much more helpful. Aces in their places.

Pro videographers capture footage and pull it all together faster and better than we can. However, I enjoy video production as a creative outlet, so I often do my own. Here is my take on several styles of short videos.

Promo Video

Let's start with a promo video for your partners. For the interview/voiceover portion, I set up a GoPro on a tripod. I'll splice in slo-mo and atmospheric elements as appropriate.

My Promo recipe:

Intro—0-3 seconds, music builds, fade to logo splash, music credit at the bottom.

First section—4-10 seconds, atmospheric beauty shots of the car with text identifying me and the partner I'm promoting.

Second section—11-18 seconds, testimonial, my voice over the race car on track and back to me.

Third section—19-26 seconds, close, details about the partner product and our association.

Outro—27-30 seconds, music fades away, my partners and my logo, then fade to black.

It takes me about two to four weeks to edit one of these. I found that hiring a pro to do a promo means I will have it back in about ten days. It's typically between $300 and $500, so it needs to be worth it. The production quality from pros is typically fantastic. You definitely get what you pay for.

Race Recap

Race recap videos are the easiest to pull together. You can upload the whole video as is. If you do, give your audience a few signposts along the way in the description. For instance, "Check out the yellow Porsche at 3:23," or "Things get interesting at 4:12!"

If you produce your race recap, pull out the bits from your race that are the most interesting and talk your audience through the race, just like an announcer. Your audience wants to hear your voice. You're telling your friends what happened. Point out how things went from calm to crazy. Put a circle around that car about to lose it, the great pass you're about to make, the tiny window you were able to fly through. All of this can be narrated by you, the driver. This doesn't have to be an Allan McNish Truth in 24 wannabe video. It can be a simple insight into the way you think on track that connects you to your followers.

You can also record your in-car communications and add it the video. It's pretty interesting to hear the crew chief and driver during the race. Add in telemetry data too. It helps your audience feel a part of the experience. There are several easy-to-use software solutions, or you can use a camera with software built in like a GoPro, AiM SmartyCam, VBox, or Garmin.

Pass Tracking

I will do this if I've improved by ten or more places during a race. This is a video of passes made. These can be super fun to cut together. Make these 60 seconds or less. It's tempting to give more flavor, but keep them short. Start the snips where you're already to their bumper. Unless there is a complicated and interesting back and forth setup to the pass, keep each one to just a few seconds each.

Team Intro

This is a behind-the-scenes video. Do an intro about what makes your team awesome and then transition into a Ken Burns-style slideshow of images. Interview teammates, show them working on the car in a high-pressure situation, cover pit stops and repairs, etc. You can even include beauty shots of the shop, the paddock setup, and the race car, and atmospheric shots of the racetrack.

Anthem Video

This is your greatest hits video. It is about the car, driver, crew, or any combination. Use it to generate interest in your team and show a potential partner the content you are capable of producing.

Anthem videos are between 30 and 60 seconds and typically feature music and engine noises. Use quick snips of video with cuts from inside to outside to panning shots, to slo-mo, to atmospheric shots. Variety helps.

The trickiest thing I've found when creating these videos is managing sound. Slo-mo footage doesn't have sound, so you fade on both sides of slo-mo. For better sound quality, try your audio from the in-car camera instead of the on-car one.

My Anthem recipe:

> Intro—0-3 seconds, music starts, my logo fades into a slo-mo of the car, music credit at bottom.
>
> First section—4-8 seconds, footage from around the race car as music builds.
>
> Second section—9-25 seconds, music fades, race car noises emphasized, music comes forward for atmospheric and slo-mo shots, transition between full speed, slo-mo, in car, and on car.
>
> Outro—26-30 seconds, fade to a splash of partner logos, music fades away to end.

Each of these videos takes me a long time to build, typically about four to six weeks to create an anthem video, two to three weeks to create a promo video, and two to four weeks to create an epic race recap.

A note on music. If you're using a song in your video, reach out to the artist and request permission to use it, especially if it's for an anthem video. Each artist has different rules regarding their art being used in promotion. There are a ton of free instrumental tracks you can get the commercial rights to if you don't want to go this route. Free is often easiest when building an anthem video.

FADE TO ORANGE

Okay, we've got the live thing down and we've got the shorter segment things down. Promos? Nailed 'em. Anthem—working on it. What else?

Find a spot close enough to capture your paddock setup process or the setup process of the whole paddock. Set up a tripod, select time-lapse, and record. Keep the camera rolling as the sun begins to set and the colors flood the sky. Move the camera if you want to get up close to the action. Shorten this time lapse to about 2-3 minutes. Record a voiceover for the video. These time-lapse videos are rarely narrated, so this is a unique touch.

You have lots of choices for time lapse or video—take a tour of the paddock on your bike, do a track walk, get creative!

PRO VIDEO FOR SALE OR RENT

If you're going to pay for video, start small. Find a photographer who wants to try out video. Hire them for the weekend—this should be in the $400-500 range. They get to learn a new skill and you get video. But keep your expectations in check with a newbie. They're learning just like you are. You may not get top quality, but you have hundreds on the line rather than thousands. As soon as you see the final product, you'll know what to do differently next time.

The typical rate for a dedicated pro videographer is quite a bit higher as it includes editing and production time. Don't be surprised at video quotes from $1,000-3,000 and higher. Video equipment is wickedly expensive.

If you do this, have a checklist for your videographer. They can do some amazing stuff like drone footage, trackside, paddock shots, grid, interviews, snippets from the radio, crew, and atmospheric stuff. Talk through the main shots you want included. Give good guidance, but don't be too prescriptive. Just describe the story you want to tell. That will go a long way towards getting you an awesome video.

14

CHOOSING ONLINE OPTIONS

It's 2017. I've just gotten back into racing.

Our national championship runoffs were at the Indianapolis Motor Speedway and we paddocked in the garages right across from the scoring pylon on the front straight, Gasoline Alley! It was amazing for a kid from Indiana to race at that historic place!

The first time out on track, I just looked at the long line of grandstands. That first time down the front straight, I could hear the expansion joint clack as I passed over the yard of bricks for the first time. I immediately keyed the mic and told my engineer how cool it was to go over the bricks.

"Focus, focus," was the reply.

The event went smoothly for my first runoffs. I came home with an 11th place finish against the best in country in my class. My race was the last race for our team. My teammates had run in another class earlier in the day. The Fiesta was sitting in the garage waiting to get loaded up onto the hauler.

A voice came from behind me. "Is this your car?" The guy was carrying what looked like a very expensive video camera. They asked if they could get some footage of the car in the garage.

"Absolutely!" was my reply. The sunset light was perfect, filtering through the grandstands into the garage and shining on the Fiesta.

They took a bunch of footage and then asked me if I would be willing to do an interview. They told me they were with Mobil 1 and that it was for Mobil 1 The Grid. They asked me several questions about Indy and why it was special to me. I told them I was turning in where my old seats used to be for the 500. As an Indiana kid, this was hallowed ground. We finished up the interview and they told me when it would air. I was super excited. I assumed the footage would make the cut. I didn't really even think about it not making the cut. Thankfully it did.

On the way home, I searched for the Mobil 1 sponsorship page and applied. This was mid-October. By late November, I hadn't heard anything. I was going to PRI in Indianapolis in early December and decided I'd see if they were there and follow up in person.

It was there I met Christian Flathman, global marketer for motorsports for Mobil 1; an awesome guy! We went up on their display stage to chat out of the way of the crowds and I explained that I met their video crew and I was interested in sponsorship from Mobil 1, but hadn't heard back.

It turned out there was a software glitch in their system that was not releasing applications to his team. As we talked, I had my back to the large display screen, and just as I was telling Christian about the video, he tapped me on the shoulder and said, "Turn around." My face was on the big screen behind me! It was a comical moment for sure. It was great to see the content had made it and would be online and on TV.

Later that afternoon, we came to a partnership agreement for the following year. Mobil 1 has been a fantastic partner, but it all started with that video crew in the garage at Indy and a conversation at PRI on the Mobil 1 stage.

LANDING SPOTS

For each of us club racers, we will have a different online presence. This is all about the fit with your brand and with your brand goals. Engaging and growing your brand online can help you spread your reach and your brand presence beyond the racetrack.

As club racers, the most important thing is this: How much is your time worth? That will truly drive the way you interact with your followers. All the online options take time to do properly.

Social media dominates the conversation space and it is important that you develop both connected and branded social media spaces. But do you need a website to support them? A website can become a central branded touchpoint for all of your social media. It can also be a home for short and longform stories about your brand.

Websites take a lot of time to set up and manage. The initial setup can take between two to three weeks. Then, it's a commitment of time each week to keep it updated and fresh. I typically spend between one and three hours a week updating the website. Good thing you have content—lots of it.

As you think about what a website can do for you and your team, draft a plan. You'll find that you can either use it and leverage it, or that it may not work for you.

Okay, so how do you do it? If you're not a website builder by trade, investigate some ready-to-go options like GoDaddy's website builder or other hosting services where they give you blocks of content to populate. This way you avoid having to become a coding expert. You can build a pretty amazing Lego-style website using the formatting tools they provide.

Depending on your skillset, you can do it yourself, or you may need to hire a web designer. This can add a whole layer of complexity and expense. Initial build fees start at $500 and there are a range of fees for routine updates.

Create a website name that matches your team name (or a shortened version of it) to make it easy for your followers to find you. You can often get a ten-year lease on the website name. I recommend this as it's way too easy to forget to renew each year and lose your domain name.

Your website says a lot about your brand, and how you approach your website can boost the strength and legitimacy of your brand. It can be a landing spot for all of your content. This is where you can go in-depth about you and your brand and how you got to where you are now. It's an opportunity to use longer form to describe the things that drive you and your brand forward.

It's also a home for an online store. You can move merchandise and develop promotions without limits on your own site. You can drive traffic from social media to your site, especially if you're doing a launch of team gear or announcing a race schedule.

It can also be a home for your blog, a place for your writing and your race recaps. It's where you can place all of your images from the race weekend. A place where you build your brand and your following by being true to you. You can use the space as an insight into your mindset and the things that drive you and build your brand backstory.

Importantly, it is a place to highlight your partners. You can spend time and energy here highlighting your partners and use this to help drive the right traffic to your partners' sites. A website can also be a showcase for your brand and your achievements.

On the flipside, a website can be a major pain in the ass to update, especially if you don't chip away at it every day. If you let it go for a length of time, you'll end up spending many hours each month instead of a few hours a week. It can get expensive too. Hosting fees for your website can be anywhere from $100-400 per year, per site.

If you can do it yourself and you have the time, and if it makes sense to support your activities, then you should have a website. A website is a great addition to your brand. It delivers a sense of legitimacy and is a great place to provide content without the limitations of social media.

YOUR FOLLOWERS HAVE MAIL

Is a mailing list right for you? It can be. You can drive followers from social media to your email list and you can drive followers from your website to your email list. But, what do you do with it?

Mailing lists connect you directly to your audience and give them a more personalized connection to you and your brand. Think of mailing lists you subscribe to and really look at why you like the ones you do.

You can use mailing lists for race recaps, sales of merch, or as a heads-up that you'll be coming to a racetrack near them. The fun thing with mailing lists is that you can create a ton of audiences and personalize the content by region, category, whatever. It's super simple to do. There are several mail list managers: MailChimp, Constant Contact, and A Weber, to name a few. Do your homework and choose what's right for you.

As with all things branding, make sure you brand your emails. Create a template with your logo and your face if you can. Be consistent. Keep the email list fonts similar to your website fonts. It should look like it is coming from the same place as all of your content.

Keep your emails short. To help with this, many services offer a shortener for emails. You write the intro to the section in your email, place a link to "read more" in the middle of a sentence, cliff-hanger style, and you've shortened your email. This gives the recipient a choice to read the rest of the story.

If your email includes several sections, shorten each section this way. Make it easy for your audience to see all the sections, like an accordion. Create the stories on your website. Then include the links to each section in your email and bring your audience to your website.

Keep up a consistent schedule of once a month to start. Brand your emails. Make them yours. Use your font and your colors. Sign them with your name. Your followers are following you, after all. Be personal. Create a short intro and exit paragraph with links to content in between. Give a quick recap of what you've done since the previous note and what's next.

Track your email performance and don't be afraid to resend your email a day later to non-openers. Use the email service's suggested send timing until you have a handle on its impact on open rates. You can experiment and see how things move as you get farther and farther into email lists.

Don't be long winded. People will tune out and TL;DR (Too Long; Didn't Read) your content. Also, don't be spammy by always asking for something. Try to balance your asks with a 4:1 ratio. Put out at least four emails about what's going on before you promote your store or ask for something. Don't use your email to fish for partners. And don't forget to send your emails. If you disappear, your open rates will go down.

Email can be a great way to introduce contests, send out goodies, etc. Have fun with them and make them work for you. Once you get going with them and have a pretty good following, you can leverage them to help extend your reach.

It takes time to create a good email following, but it's worth building the connection with your brand. Think of the cool emails from lists that you subscribe to that make you think, "Hey, I wonder what's up with them this week?" It makes for a nice diversion from the everyday.

MANAGING YOUR SOCIAL MEDIA

We've got content, we've got a brand voice, now let's build a social media personality for our brand. With social media, you can extend the reach of your brand beyond the track to reach anyone in the world. This is easy to do through Facebook, Instagram, LinkedIn and others. Sign up for a business page for your team and connect your personal page as page manager. Each social media service has a different way of doing this, so just follow their directions.

Take your time and brand your pages. Use your logo and use an image of you that is easily recognizable. Embrace your colors; give it the fully branded experience. Have a consistent profile picture across your networks. This profile picture should be a professional headshot. Use a consistent background and team or personal brand description across all your social media sites to make it easy for people to find you.

In the description, fill out your team story, your location, and a way to contact you. All of this can be changed later, so it doesn't have to be perfect right away. The only thing that is a bit tricky to edit is the name. Try to get your team name, obviously. If it is already taken, then add something to it that makes it unique. For instance, if Ollie Rocket Racing had been taken, we would have chosen Ollie Rocket Racing—Michigan or something like that to identify us.

You will also be given the option to create a vanity URL. Do this. Try to make this tag the same across all the social media platforms you use. It makes it so much easier for people to find you when you are consistent across services.

If you choose to update your profile or background pictures, tread carefully. The more consistent and familiar you are, the better. If you do choose to do this from time to time, have a reason for the change. Then, update each of your personal brand sites at the same time. You can play around with home and away profile pictures if you're going to your home track or to travel tracks. You could use a dark and light profile picture background and the appropriate logo for each. Doesn't matter. Have a reason.

TONE, TONE, TONE

For some, social media becomes a chore. For others, it's a fun way of letting friends know what you're up to. You know where on this continuum you lie based on your own personal social media habits. This one you don't have to figure out.

Dig in and embrace your brand and deliver the branded experience your fans, followers, and partners expect. Some of us will not have time during a race weekend and will need to have someone do it for us. A virtual assistant may be an affordable option for managing your social media and website. Make sure they capture your tone and voice.

Tone is critical to get right as so much of social media is text based. You are speaking, you are living your brand at the track, and connecting with your followers on a more personal level.

Strive to do your best to be true to your brand tone online. Think about the Old Spice and Wendy's examples from earlier. Maintain that consistent voice and tone across your social media. Hold your brand to that standard in all of your social posts.

When responding to your followers' comments on posts, be prompt and respectful and above all be on brand. If your brand is a little snarky, then embrace the snark, but do it with respect. Your partners and followers will likely see all of your content and responses, so choose wisely. If you make a brand failure mistake, take it down quickly and apologize. We all make mistakes and our apologies go a long way to fixing them.

YOU ARE THE FACE OF YOUR BRAND

If you are working on your own personal brand on social media, then sign up for an athlete page and follow the same path—consistent brand, background, team colors, the works.

You can also investigate building a public figure page for your personal brand. This is separate from your personal social media and is solely focused on you as an athlete and a brand. One of the benefits of a public figure page is that you can ultimately grow your following larger than you can on your personal social media page due to follower limits. You can also be more selective in what you post there.

When developing your personal club racing social media brand, separate from the team brand, you need to put your face out there. I know I'm banging on a bit about this, but your brand starts with you and your face and your personality. Your profile picture for your personal brand page should be a picture of you. The background picture can be your race car, the transporter, team colors, or logo, but the profile picture across all of your personal brand social media should be the same picture of your face.

Keeping this profile image consistent across platforms makes it easier for people to find you. If they are looking for you on a different platform, you want them to be able to recognize you from your profile picture. Think of your personal brand page as your best foot forward, your introduction to the club racing world. One benefit of being consistent is that you can copy and paste descriptions from platform to platform and only make edits for space constraints.

One of the more powerful networking tools recently is LinkedIn. Many racers, both pro and grassroots, are turning to LinkedIn to extend their networks beyond the racetrack. As you interact and grow your personal network through LinkedIn, you can grow your club racing brand as well.

It is fairly easy to build your network through LinkedIn. You never know where conversations on there will lead. Be valuable to your connections and be a light for grassroots racers.

INVITE YOUR FRIENDS

In several social media services, you can invite your personal connections to follow your team and personal branded pages. This is an easy way to jumpstart your following on social media. One caution, though: for most of these services, you can only invite people once. There are a few ways to maximize this. At first, when you have very few followers, it works well to give a heads-up to your friends on your personal social media that you are going to invite them to like your team or personal brand page.

Once you've gathered a few hundred followers, then invite a group of 25-50 friends per day to like your page. The more people like your page, the more likely others will like it as well.

You can also send out a reminder post on your personal social media. Just don't make it needy or beg. Make it more of a "Hey, check out our racing page and follow us to see what we're doing throughout the season" kind of thing. It's easy to just click invite all, but I have found that a quick note followed up with the normal invite gets a better response.

Also, for high-engagement posts, especially those that have been shared widely, look though the likes and invite people who liked your post who are not already your followers. This is an easy way to include more people in your circle and provide them with more insight into your team. They liked your post, so it's okay to invite them to like your brand. You'll be surprised how quickly you can grow your following this way.

THE LONG GAME

You've created a strong brand, you've breathed life into it and you've created awesome content, now it's time to put all of this to use to grow your presence on social media. It's time to dedicate a little money each day to grow your brand. Social media has very low organic reach rates, so a little targeted spend can be a good investment in increasing reach and engagement for your brand.

It doesn't have to be expensive. You can build a social media ad and run it every day over the course of the year. These brand-building ads run for as little as $1 per day. You can spend as much as you like, but start small and see what happens over the first couple of months. You may want to refine your audience targets and re-do the ad.

So, what should your ad be? It should be a call to action to like and follow your racing page. If this is for the team, you're asking people to follow you on your journey throughout the season. If you're using video, it should be inspirational and interesting, and under 45 seconds if possible. Use your anthem video if you've created it already. If you're using photos, make sure to include your team logo, a picture of the cars, and the whole team.

Take a close look at ads that come across your feed asking the same thing. Know what gets you to follow and what you skip. Each series will have its unique hooks. Don't rush into getting your ad out. Work on the language and imagery until you're happy.

The next step is to define your target audience. You get to define it, which is awesome! Who do you want to follow you? What interests do you think they might have? Start with what you know—your form of motorsports (motocross, drag racing, off-road, karting, road racing, etc.), add in your specific series, your town or city, your state, then take a look at ages.

What age ranges do you want to follow you? This will be different for each series. I typically include all ranges until I see the first month's results of the ad and then adjust the target audience accordingly. One of the cool things about this is after a few adjustments, you can kind of set it and forget it. Let the ad run and continually bring in new followers from your target audience each month.

As you get more confident with your ad, you may want to up the spend a bit near the beginning or middle of the season. Be cautious as it can sometimes be easy to lose track of your social media ad spend when an ad is running continuously.

15

SOCIAL MEDIA POSTING SCHEDULES

It's early 2009 and we're in the middle of the 2010 Mustang launch.

We completed all the tease elements and we had the big reveal at Barker Hanger before the LA Auto Show. We were filling in the space between the November 2008 reveal and the start of production in spring of 2009.

We developed a campaign around the theme of 2010 by asking our Mustang enthusiasts to tell us how they would unleash their inner Mustang. We called it '10 Unleashed.

This idea of the unleashing the inner Mustang side came from research early in 2008. We asked customers how they felt when they got in their Mustang. Responses varied from putting on a suit of armor to putting on red high heels. At each research event, we continued to get these kinds of responses from our Mustang customers, both men and women.

The best ideas for the '10 Unleashed would be featured in the campaign. We received thousands of responses from our passionate fans. These included teaching a blind driver to do donuts, taking a Mustang rallying, drag racing a student vs. a teacher where the winner gets the car, teaching celebrities to race, rail grinding a mustang in a skate park, and a slew of other amazing experiences for our customers.

We planned to kick off the '10 Unleashed by going big. Japan big. We flew Vaughn Gittin Jr. and a specially prepared drift Mustang to Tokyo. We were sending Vaughn to one of the original homes of drifting—the Bihoku Highland Drifting circuit.

We wanted to do some underground promotion for this event ahead of time. We asked the agency for tens of thousands of Mustang Drift Japan stickers to be created. We intended to send packs of these stickers to all our Mustang Club members across the country and around the world.

Timing was essential. We were going to be very quiet about the Mustang Drift Japan launch of the '10 Unleashed campaign until the video was released on YouTube. We needed these Mustang Drift Japan stickers at least six weeks ahead of time so we could get them out into the world and generate conversation about what the heck is Mustang Drift Japan.

It was the final extension of the '10 Mustang's tease campaign. We figured six weeks would be enough time to catch people's attention across the country and start a conversation. Our plan was to have our Mustang Club friends place these stickers on their toolboxes, on lampposts, at race tracks, wherever they wanted to.

This was an homage to Shepard Fairey's Andre the Giant OBEY stickers back in the late 80s and early 90s. The ones that showed up everywhere as part of one of the very first viral campaigns. We were going for something similar, so the sticker design was minimal. It had a dark gray background, a lighter gray image of the country of Japan, the Kanji symbol for Japan in red, and the English words Mustang Drift in white at the bottom. Simple, a little mysterious, but effective.

The goal was to get the stickers out there, get the word out there something was happening. We planned to include a note in each sticker pack asking them to send in their best picture of the sticker placed somewhere, anywhere. We were going to quietly give the 10-12 people who sent in the coolest pictures of our stickers in unusual locations a supercool Mustang-themed reward.

As we were closing in on our six-week deadline, we could not get the agency to finalize the sticker design. No matter how many times we stressed the timing. We had to have the stickers in our hands at least six weeks before the team left for Japan.

The combination of the very difficult logistics for the Japan trip and the bureaucracy inside the agency kept slowing down decision making. Ultimately, unfortunately, the stickers were delivered to our office the same week the team left for the Japan trip.

We had long since given up on the viral campaign element of the stickers and they were relegated to handouts at various enthusiast events. What could have been an awesome and underground tease ended up being sub-optimal at best. Perhaps if we had come up with the idea earlier or imposed a much earlier deadline, things could have been different. As it was, Mustang Drift Japan was pretty awesome on its own, but we had an opportunity to turn it up to 11.

Timing matters.

TIMING TIPS

One of the cool things about social media business pages is that you can schedule when you want your posts to hit your page. Use this feature to enhance visibility and engagement with your posts.

The time you post impacts the reach you have, and the people who see and interact with your posts. Each social media platform has different times where posts are most seen, engaged with, and shared. This changes over time depending on the platform. When you are getting started with your team's social media, it may be helpful to compare online sources for the best timing for Facebook, Instagram, LinkedIn, Snapchat and others.

This does change over time, but the rule of thumb is that Facebook and Instagram tend to be most viewed and engaged with towards the end of the work day and over the weekend. LinkedIn has an unusual engagement pattern as it's a network primarily used by professionals. It has its highest engagement from Tuesday through Thursday around lunchtime and mid-afternoon.

Another way to increase the likelihood that your friends and followers will engage with your posts on Facebook and Instagram is to use the stories feature. This will place your post in a queue at the top of their feed. It doesn't guarantee engagement, but it does increase the likelihood of your fans and followers seeing and engaging with your post.

Social media audiences and platforms evolve quickly. Use your insights data to understand when your followers are online and engaged, and try to place your posts during these times for the best connection with your followers. Combine this with your learning about typical patterns for each platform and schedule your posts during these times.

HAPPY EASTER, EASTER BUNNY, BAWK BAWK!

As club racers, we all know how crazy things can get during the lead-up to an event, during the event itself, and while packing up to get home. You will often run out of time to create a well-worded post with great imagery.

How do you find the time? Create a calendar of post ideas. Create the posts and schedule them for automatic posting when you're super busy. You don't have to think about it during the last-minute chaos of packing.

This works especially well for holiday posts like Memorial Day, July 4th, birthdays of crew members, or just about any special occasion. Set aside some time to create these posts and schedule them to go out during high-engagement times just before or on the holiday itself. These are set it and forget it posts and you'll be amazed how spending some dedicated time creating a dozen or more scheduled posts will free you up from the everyday posting mania on social media.

Get organized with a posting calendar. Place a number of posts in the queue to supplement the more organic ones at and around race weekends. Include a short blurb about each post subject on the calendar and a note as to whether you've created and scheduled it yet. The farther you plan out, the more consistent and more cohesive your social media presence becomes.

It will feel like a lot of work during downtime at first. Use the tools you have available to you and take short blocks of time to craft several posts at once across several platforms. As you get comfortable with post scheduling, you will realize it frees up time to get on with the business of racing when you need it most.

How frequently should you post? Three times a week is a good guideline to make sure you are appearing on your follower's feeds. If your brand is more engaging, by all means schedule more posts per week and weekend. And, even though you're using scheduled posts, keep giving your followers updates throughout the race weekend adventure.

PEOPLE PROFILES

Teammate profiles are great for pre-populated posts! It's an awesome way to introduce your team to your friends, fans, and followers. These are fun to do and give a little behind-the-scenes detail on each of your teammates and crew. You'll find that sharing one or two of these a weekend is a super-fun diversion from race car pictures.

To highlight your individual crew members, write a short bio, how you met, and a thank you. Then, when you have the right photography, add the picture to each pre-created post and schedule it. People profiles tend to be well shared and have high engagement.

EVERYTHING ELSE IS WAITING

So, it's between race weekends. What do you want to do to engage with your fans, friends, and followers? Here are a few ideas that have worked for us.

You can showcase prepping the car, repairing the car, loading the car, and loading the trailer. People are often amazed at how much stuff it takes to go racing and this is a good way to show them.

I do partner spotlights once a week or month. I learned this from sprint car driver Stu Snyder of SLS Motorsports. We create a template with a distinctive background. We add in a large hi-res picture of our race car with our partner's logo featured. Then, on the side in quoted text, include a quote from the driver about why the partner or the partner's product is awesome. It is our way of giving back to our partners.

For other between race weekend posts, think of what's next and highlight it. Include your points standing, an image of the car or the driver, what you love about the next track or race you're headed to. If you've been there before, how did you do last time?

Put up some whimsical posts about how you wish you could get back to the racetrack. Have fun! It's whatever you think of when you're not at the track and wish you were. It could be you sitting in the race car and staring out the windshield at the back garage wall, wishing it was the track. It could be the smell of race gas in the morning. It could be imagining your neighborhood as a race track. Do what strikes you. The great thing is all of these can be scheduled far in advance so you can set it and forget it with these.

RACE WEEKEND MADNESS!

Posts during race weekends are probably the most difficult to find time for, but you need to. Help your future self out here and write out your partner thank yous and hashtags ahead of time. Save them in a file that you can get to easily. I save mine in my Notes on my iPhone.

Do five or six versions of these, number them, and use a different one each time. You may need to relink the tags. You won't have to worry that you'll forget to mention one of your partners—one of our big worries as drivers. Before you post, paste in the copy you've already written out.

When you finish your session, get a drink, get settled, and take five minutes to give your fans and followers a quick update. The memories are fresh and your post will be authentic. Then get changed and get to work on the car. With a little practice, you'll find that these five minutes will be super effective.

Okay, you've finished the last session of the weekend and you've made it back from impound to your paddock spot. You've cooled off and you're ready to load up the car to get home. Take a pause and give yourself some after-session time to drop a post.

This time you're going to need about ten minutes though. A full weekend recap should include a race recap of what just happened and a short recap of your adventures throughout the weekend. Again, do it while it's fresh in your mind. I try to do this before I get changed out of my suit. Once I'm out of my suit, I'm getting the car loaded and getting everything packed up, saying bye to friends, and all of the thousand other things we do before leaving.

BRUSH YOUR TEETH

Everything gets easier once it becomes a habit. Social media is no different. It can be a bit of a pain as you try to get your five minutes after each session when you know there are things to be done on the car. But if you dive right into working on the car, your post will disappear under the time pressure.

Get in this habit. It's five minutes. Know what you're going to say and get it done. You'll find that the more you do this, the easier it becomes. Pretty soon, you'll do it out of routine and you'll keep your followers engaged and up to date throughout the weekend.

Use your pre-typed tags and thank you notes to save effort, but take the time you need to get these updates out. It really does become easier to budget the time once you build it into your schedule. This is no different to taking your time while changing from your suit into your street clothes.

NEED A LITTLE HELP HERE!

At some point, your club racing team is going to grow. It will get to the point that you're going to need someone to manage the team's social media. If you can no longer take the time to post during the race weekend and you find your race weekend time consumed with partner meetings, leading your team, and getting the cars out on track, then maybe it is time to investigate adding a social media person. While this seems crazy, it is actually a good thing.

For me, it's all about time. What is my time best used for? If I have available time, I'm doing my own social media. If I'm skipping after-session updates and only have time to post at the end of each day, I might need to delegate the responsibility. I weigh the potential for off-brand posts against sub-optimal posting schedules.

You can do this a few ways if you're not able to give your social media the time it needs. You can add social media responsibilities to one of your crew's duties. Try to choose someone who can focus on building and publishing stories while you are on track or just off track. Your brand voice and tone are important. Make sure that they have this down just right.

Another way to think about it is hiring someone specifically to be your social media person. Social media specialists can certainly bring out more team stories and create more content. If you are running out of time and you have the funds, then it could be for you. Just make sure you can guide the tone and voice with a strong hand at first until they understand you.

PART IV

BUILDING PARTNERSHIPS

16

HOW TO FIND PARTNERS

It's spring of 1994. We've crashed once and won three times in the ITC Civic.

Toyo supplied all the tires we needed through their generous contingency program. I was having trouble affording the mount and balance fees for the tires, so I approached our local Toyo tire dealer and tire shop, Paul Williams Tire (PWT).

I was getting all of my contingency tires delivered to PWT to begin with, so the owner knew me as that racer guy who keeps on winning tires. I think we got a full set for each win. We racked up a dozen wins that year and ended up with more tires than we could ever use! I asked if they'd be interested in a partnership where I promoted their shop and they helped me with mounting tires.

Things started out great. I provided PWT with a team picture and updated them after every race. They helped me by mounting and balancing and getting rid of old tires. Things were great throughout the summer. I talked about them and sent friends and family in the area their way.

As the summer progressed, I thought of ways to do even more for my first real partner in the sport. I brought racer friends to PWT and PWT offered them a small discount. In my mind, this was more business for PWT and more validation that I was being a good partner.

Unbeknownst to me, some of my racer friends were taking a bit too much advantage of this arrangement and began bringing in way more tires than PWT had time to do during a day. PWT still had their regular customers to take care of. They made way more money on oil changes, suspension, and exhaust work than they did mounting and balancing tires.

The guys at PWT pulled me aside and asked me to back off on the friends and family deal. They didn't want to do that much mounting and balancing. I understood, and I offered to buy the staff pizza the next day as a thank you for all of their hard work. They told the guys that pizza was coming the next day.

Fate stepped in. Overnight, I came down with the flu. I called in sick to work and lay in bed like we all do when we're super sick. I completely forgot about my responsibility to feed the guys at PWT. At about 2 PM, I sat straight up in bed—oh crap!

I called them and apologized. They said they understood, but the relationship was never the same. They never said it out loud, but I had dropped the ball and they didn't have time for people who dropped the ball. I let them down and this partnership was becoming a distraction. PWT stayed as a partner through the 1994 season and we agreed not to renew for 1995. When I think back, it was that dropped ball that changed the dynamics of the relationship.

I have taken that experience and lesson into every one of my partnerships since. When working with my partners, I do my damndest to deliver on my promises and help them achieve their goals. I make it easy for them to be proud of our partnership.

Fast forward to 2018 and PRI. I set up a meeting with Mark Link from Frozen Rotors. Little did I know at the time that this 45-minute meeting at a high-top table in the food court at the Indianapolis Convention

Center in the middle of PRI would become one of my longest-lasting partnerships.

Mark and I talked about his goals for his company, what he was looking for in a partner, why he wanted to meet with me, and what I had that he needed help with. It came down to this: Mark needed to get the brand name out there and he needed content, video, and imagery to support his marketing efforts.

On the flipside, I was going through rotors every other race and it was getting expensive. Frozen Rotors were durable enough to last most of the season. We each had something the other needed.

I focused on overdelivering on our agreement for Mark. I set out to make Mark proud of our partnership and to make it easy to re-up year over year. I keep my commitments to Mark no matter what and we continue helping each other grow our presence in the sport.

There will be no pizza shortage this time. I cringe every time I think of the guys at PWT waiting for pizza to show and then no pizza, then lunchtime is over and grumpy, hungry guys go back to work only to be fed at their toolboxes later in the afternoon. Never again. Promises made are promises kept.

YOU DON'T SELL EXPOSURE

Full credit for this idea to the fabulous book by Alex Striller on motorsports marketing. Alex's *Motorsports Marketing and Sponsorships—How to Raise Money to Race and Give Sponsors What They Really Want* has been my go-to for marketing my team and for building and promoting my corporate partnerships. The key challenge that he talks about is that cost of exposure has fallen through the floor. Even several years after its first printing, the lesson rings true. For less than $100 a month, any company can build an online campaign targeted towards a specific customer set and easily achieve 20k views per month of exposure.

Marketers are smart. They have a limited amount of money and they have a clear set of goals they need to achieve. Some companies desperately want exposure and they want it quickly. Unfortunately, as a club racing marketing platform, we aren't efficient in providing exposure. The exposure numbers we provide can't compete with a corporate Amazon, Google, or Facebook ad. Heck, they probably can't compete with a billboard.

As a marketing platform, we club racers don't sell exposure anymore. We just don't.

Each motorsport is different. Even for those with weekly audiences in the stands, this rule still applies. It's hard to compete here on reach alone.

This is a bit of a downer as we all have social media metrics and audience demographics at our fingertips. Unfortunately, we cannot lean on these to sell space on the car to generate exposure for our partners.

Of course, partners will get their logos on the car, but exposure in the normal sense is more of a check-the-box exercise than anything. It's a different world now. The space on the car, the space on the driver's suit, and the space on the hauler is not the primary benefit.

This doesn't mean that we no longer offer exposure to our partners; we certainly do, absolutely. We just don't make it the central part of our pitch to our partners. We are going to focus instead on how to help them market their products and grow their sales. We're going to do it with different tools than we have used in the past. As a matter of fact, we can do something that corporate Facebook or Google or even billboard advertising cannot.

We are going to sell authenticity and build connections for our partners. We can deliver marketing messages to our followers with our unique brand perspective and personality. This is something that no corporate marketer can do. It's the Holy Grail of word of mouth and viral advertising that every corporate marketer wishes they could tap into. This is why we worked to build a brand authentic to us that speaks with our voice and personality.

Marketing teams constantly seek to elevate the authenticity of their brand. This is why you see companies link themselves with celebrities they believe fit with or enhance their brand. Over time, the celebrity is asked to speak more and more corporately. Ultimately, their referral power and the reason the company connected with them in the first place is degraded.

Think about times where you were at an amateur sporting event and a corporate presence was totally over the top. It was obvious that they were buying their way into the event. This is where we win as club racers. We are a promotional voice for our partners in spaces where corporate messages ring hollow.

We lift our partner brands up with our authentic voice and connect with customers on a personal level. We sell authenticity. We connect large brands with grassroots competitors in a grassroots environment and we open doors that they are unable to credibly open on their own.

SELL YOUR PRODUCT

As we think of what we can provide for our partners, it helps to think of ourselves and our team as a product. Thank you to Enzo Mucci and his phenomenal book, *Get the Drive: The Only Way to Get Motorsport Sponsorship Now*, for that concept. We are indeed selling a product and our product is us—our team.

Our team and our marketing efforts are a product. Our potential partners are using their precious marketing dollars to buy something. It's critical we understand what they want to buy. Our funding ask might sometimes feel like a bit of a rounding error in the grand scheme of things. It isn't. Smart marketers combine all of those rounding errors to do more with the limited funds available to them. Let's find a way to help them buy our product.

Finding partnerships takes a lot of time and effort. Start with endemic companies. Companies that make their living off motorsports and specifically our form of motorsport. In karting, this might be a local kart shop, a specific bearing company, or a kart wheel company. In road racing, this might be a tire, shock, or brake company.

The company is invested in motorsports and familiar with the benefits motorsports can bring. As you look to partner with endemic companies, understand the value you and your product can bring. Ask questions, understand their marketing objectives. Figure out where your capabilities and their objectives overlap. That's your sweet spot and your "in" to begin the conversation about a potential partnership.

How do you find the ones that need the help you can provide? Do your homework on each one that you are interested in. You may find that some companies like Mobil 1 invest in racing from grassroots to Sprint Cars to NASCAR to F1 to show the breadth of their product capabilities. You may find that some companies only support pro levels of competition or only support certain series and don't want to play in others.

Understand where they play now. Are they title sponsors for events, teams, or individuals? Are they contingency sponsors? How do they advertise and what events do they support? The answers will prepare you for your initial conversations.

Non-endemic companies seem more difficult to approach. It's your job to show the benefit that the motorsport environment can provide. Is it an opportunity to network outside of the office in a fun environment? Is it a new angle and a new vision for one of their brands? Understand their challenges and their marketplace before you engage them. Be a knowledgeable ambassador for motorsports and highlight yourself as an authentic marketing partner.

There are more partnership opportunities out there than you realize. Focus on the ones that value grassroots and what the little guy can bring to the table. Use your tools and your expertise to bring options they might not have considered. Know your audience of followers, fans, and friends. Your followers can be a potential customer base and can advocate for your partners.

Can you help increase sales to justify their investment in you and your team each year? Show your value in the areas they care about. Help them where they need help, not only where you're good at helping. Make sure you understand their business challenges and how you can help them solve their issues. A pizza company doesn't really care how good you are at setting up ladders.

RESEARCH, RESEARCH, RESEARCH

Do your homework before you approach a partner for the first time. Approach each company as a consultant would. What's their market? Who are their competitors? What is their annual revenue? How much do they spend on marketing and advertising? Are they an up-and-coming competitor, a seasoned vet? What have they been doing to market their product over the past 12 months?

Figure out why they play in each space. Know everything you can about their challenges if you are to help them going forward. Sometimes, this is impossible as they do little to no advertising. This is totally ok. Make a list of questions to ask when you are in that first meeting.

This is a bit of a controversial one, but you can reach out to a potential partner's competitors and customers and find out what they think of the company. You don't need to mention sponsorship or racing, you're just doing research. Go on the Better Business Bureau site and see the comments. Go to recommendations sites like Google, Yelp, Angi, etc. Read the reviews.

If they spend little to no money on marketing, then they may not be a good candidate for a partnership. If they only support professional teams, then they may not want to work with a grassroots team. For every one partner that agrees to sit down with you, you may contact 20-40 that won't. This can be dispiriting, but keep your focus.

ASK QUESTIONS

You've done your homework. You've researched potential partners, and you've landed your first meeting. Now what? Why did they agree to take time to chat with you and explore a potential partnership? Boy Scout Motto here: Be Prepared. You want to understand their motivations right out of the gate. In that first meeting you want to know more about them than they do about you. They will try to do the same.

It will seem weird to do this, but ask them directly why they chose to sit down with you. Ask them what kind of help they are looking for. You may not be the only motorsport group they're talking to, so this is a good way to get a clear understanding of their expectations fast.

It's way too easy to fall into the trap of telling them what we can do and failing to listen to what our partner wants from us. In that first get-to-know-you period, focus on learning. Ask lots of questions. They may think that all motorsports have the same impact as F1 and NASCAR. This is a good time to get this out on the table and reinforce your status as a very good marketer who competes in grassroots motorsport.

It is critical that you understand your partner's marketing goals. Is it increased sales, increased value for their brand, increased reach, new markets? Is it access to your other partners as potential business opportunities? Is it access to the paddock and potential business opportunities with other companies that sponsor racing?

By doing your homework and asking your partners for their marketing goals and objectives, you can build structure around a partnership program that will work for both of you.

WHO'S BRINGING THE CHIPS?

This is probably the most difficult part of developing a new partner relationship. How do you value your grassroots product and how does a potential partner value your product? Are they similar?

You, as a grassroots competitor, may tend to see yourself at the lower end of the spectrum of providing value for sponsorship products. Don't. You've built an amazing brand! You've put your soul into your brand and your brand brings value to anyone associated with you. You just need to figure out how to quantify the value of your brand.

This is a truly tricky bit. It helps to step back. You've had the conversation with your potential partner and they've identified things they think you can help with and you're focused on those things. Try this. Ask them what they would spend to get the same results by going through a mainstream marketing effort. Then ask them where they would like to be with you.

Keep in mind that brand authenticity, a credible voice on the inside of things, is part of what they're buying. Remember, that's part of why they are talking to you. Think of yourself as their grassroots brand ambassador. You can help them extend their brand into your space. What is your brand authenticity worth? What is sharing a part of your brand worth?

Next, think about how much time and money will it cost you to activate your potential partner's brand. Activation encompasses your onsite and online extension of their brand into the grassroots racing space. In essence, this is how you promote their brand.

Let's start online and work towards at-track activation. Everybody is at a different level in motorsports. Some club racers can do full-blown track hospitality and some arrive in an open trailer. This doesn't matter in the online space. At all.

Let's use social media advertising as an example of online activation. You can place a social media ad for as little as a dollar a day. That's the lower limit. We're going to be an authentic voice for our partners in this space, work with them to create a targeted audience, and amplify their brand goals. If a social media presence is one of the things they are looking for you to enhance, like in this example, make sure you put a dollar amount against this effort. Commit 5-10% of the cash funding to your branded ads for them.

Quality content is not free. This is where you can get creative though. You can offer to come to the company's place and have them shoot a promo with you. You can offer to have them come out to the track to do the same. Also, you can pay to create one for them. If you do this, make sure you charge for the videographer plus a little additional for your time.

If they are after at-track hospitality, make sure you can deliver. This can be time consuming. If you are going to do hospitality, tickets, giveaways, or any other promotional items, you need to build those costs into your proposal. At-track activation will be driven by their marketing goals. Your job is to deliver on the awesomeness you promise.

I think you'll be surprised how much value you can bring to the table for your partners. As you build your plan, itemize these things. Don't underprice activation. At-track activation can be expensive. Whether it is handing out promotional merchandise or creating a branded space, make sure you know the costs before you commit. Remember what they said they would spend to get the same results through a mainstream marketing effort. You don't want to lose money on a partnership because you didn't fully account for your own activation costs.

DO NOT OVERCOMMIT. ALWAYS OVERDELIVER.

This should probably be printed in bold letters all over the front of the book. This is the most important part of building a lasting partnership. We all want to please our partners. As a club racer, this isn't our full-time job, though. So, balance your time commitments appropriately.

When you promise, you MUST deliver.

When we as grassroots racers enter into an agreement with a partner, we commit ourselves to delivering value. Think about hiring somebody to cut your grass. If they promised to edge the sidewalks, pull weeds, and bag all the clippings as part of the deal, then you would expect that. Too often those first few experiences will be great. But after a while they forget to bag the clippings or skip edging one week. Pretty quickly you're asking yourself, "What am I paying them for again?"

Deliver what you promise and go above by 10-15%. If you've promised hospitality at the track, surprise them with great wine or their favorite beer. Reward them for making a great decision to partner with you. If you host them at the track, fill their time with fantastic experiences. If you've promised networking for them and they're the only partner able to come that weekend, find a way to introduce them to other teams and drivers. Find a way to overdeliver.

The hardest thing about all of this is doing it week after week. One way to keep track of your deliverables is to write them down. Make a checklist for each of your partners. Your partners are experiencing your awesomeness and you need to keep the awesomeness at the same level from start to finish.

In this business, especially at the club level, the main value our partners see in supporting our passion is very specific to them. Every partner has a different reason to connect with motorsports. Think about it from their perspective and help them justify the expense of supporting your team.

Remember that we don't sell exposure. We sell experiences, networking, branding, authenticity, and a whole list of other things corporate partners are looking for.

It is easy to get carried away during the what-are-you-looking-for portion of the pitch and start saying "We can do that!" to every idea they throw out. You may find that each individual element is completely doable, but delivering all of these elements at once may be sub-optimal at best.

It's also an opportunity to talk about what you do for your existing partners. You can show what you are currently doing, highlighting your capabilities while giving them a sense of what's already on your plate. Most of us ask for a lot during negotiations and expect to be pulled back. They will too. By explaining your current commitments, you help them get a better handle on your ability to serve them properly.

You can also ask them for help in delivering the partnership goals. Let's say social media is critical to them. You may be thinking that you will need to hire a dedicated social media person just to handle this partner. Why not ask if they would be willing to send one of their own social media team to support you at the track?

You'll be surprised by their reaction—you've just offered to help them increase their footprint through authentic content that they can control. You're integrating them into your program. Be creative and open doors for them that they never knew existed.

BE OKAY WITH NO

This is a difficult one. Be okay when they say no. More importantly, be okay when you say no. Let's take that last one first. When do you say no to a potential partner?

Look at what you're being asked to do through the lens of under promise but overdeliver. As you bring new partners to your team, focus on growing your partners together. This should not be zero-sum where one grows at the expense of the others. Can you take care of this potential partner without jeopardizing your existing ones? If the answer is no, talk about it. If it's a deal breaker for the potential partner, adjust how you work with your existing ones or be ok with no.

Sometimes the math doesn't add up and it's ok to say no in those cases. When a partnership discussion feels too one-sided, try to right it and stress the value you bring to the table. Highlight each element of the program that has cost in time and money. Yes, we can absolutely do X, Y, and Z, but X costs this much, Y costs this much, and Z costs this much. Then, you can approach things from a menu perspective and help them understand the time and money value of each element.

Ultimately, if you don't have the same expectations, try to leave the discussion with a win for both of you. If there is another team that you think could benefit from working with them as a partner, offer to connect them. It never hurts to help others. You may not be able or willing to do what they are looking for, but someone else might be. Leave things on a good note.

You are going to get the "No" answer as well. You are going to find what looks like the perfect potential partner, approach them, have a great meeting, and walk away thinking, "Here we go!" Then a week passes and you reach back out to discover that they've chosen another path. It happens.

Be ok with "No". If they'll let you, treat it as an exit interview. Ask if there was something they needed that you couldn't provide and ask if you can come back to them next year.

You will go through stretches when it feels like every potential partner you approach says no or declines to meet. Stick with it. It's all part of the game. Do research on yourself, and learn what is working during your pitches and what is not.

Developing new partnerships takes a lot of time. Above all, be resilient and bounce back from rejection. Keep your chin up and keep on researching companies. The right partnerships exist and you will find them. You will walk in and it will be like magic. We need this—yep, we do that—we need this other thing—yep, we do that too. And you're off to the races!

17

EMBRACE PRODUCT PARTNERSHIPS

It's 2016. I'm getting back into club racing after several years off.

I purchased the Fiesta and designed the livery. I was a little rusty, so I started out small and reached out to a friend who runs a photography business taking portrait pictures for seniors, families, kids, and graduations.

The business was called MMB Imagery and Michelle Massey Barnes (MMB) knew little about racing, but she's a phenomenal photographer. She knows light and has been taking pictures of Will and our family since Will was born.

I approached Michelle and asked her to meet for coffee. We spent a lot of time talking about how racing worked and potential opportunities for a portrait photographer at racetracks like shooting paddock scenes and driver headshots. She was interested and Michelle soon became the first partner in this next chapter of my racing.

Michelle's business is a very small one and they rely solely on word of mouth. As a grassroots marketer, word of mouth is one of the things I am good at. It seemed like a great fit. We talked through how typical partnerships work and I put forward a number.

Cash funding wasn't going to work for her, but for me, if we didn't have to spend on our twice a year pictures, so it would be like getting funding. Also, if I could use Michelle's images to grow our presence online and in the paddock, that would help us too. I valued our package at about $2,500 per year of product sponsorship. I would provide word-of-mouth advertising for Michelle across our social media platforms and at our local tracks. In return, she would provide imagery free of charge to me and my team.

MMB Imagery would become the 2017 title sponsor for the car. This seems like a lot of exposure for a little bit of spend, but we had a plan. I told her I needed a partner's branding on the car and that once other partners came along that were willing to spend more, I would move her branding to a less prominent location.

Marketing and branding is often all about creating impressions. A title sponsor for our team generated a sense of confidence when talking with new partners and helped us gain credibility. We weren't an unbranded vehicle any more. If MMB Imagery partnered with us, then it was okay for others to do the same.

Every few months, Michelle and I would meet to see how things were working. I'd align our promotions with her objectives and keep on going. Michelle and her son loved coming to the track and cheering on their race car. I introduced Michelle to other racers who wanted headshots and paddock imagery. We received so many great images from that first season on track.

As the season progressed, Michelle and I discussed how well the partnership was working. We were generating business for her, but being away on race weekends was costing her revenue back at the studio. It was one of those unintended consequences of opportunity costs.

Sure, we could grow her business, but the growth we delivered was less profitable and more time-consuming than her existing client load. Fun, yes, but making her less money.

This marked a pivot in our relationship. I shifted our promotion from at-track photography to enhancing the strength of her brand promise. I pushed clients to her studio and backed off on the at-track promotion. Our partnership has evolved every year and MMB Imagery is one of my longest-lasting partnerships. We still promote her business locally and she still helps us with our family photography. One of my favorites was a session with Will and I both in our driver's suits and helmets—so cool.

This first product partnership created a foundation for the rest of our partnerships. If I had held out for cash funding, it wouldn't have happened. The product partnership we have developed helps both of us. Michelle gets great and unusual images for her site, and we do too.

This focus on product partnerships over paid partnerships sets the groundwork for future funded partnerships. To this day, I support Michelle and her brand because her partnership was the foundation we built our program around.

DRESS YOUR CAR FOR SUCCESS

We've all been there: a naked car. Our paint scheme carefully designed, lettered, and numbered, our contingency partners on the fender or door. The rest is blank, unsponsored. Sure, it would be great to have Kellogg's, DuPont, or Bass Pro Shop on the side of the car, but no. It sits there, looking plain.

Start small. For most companies, the appeal of supplying product is that they can do it at their cost, which is far less than the retail price. They also don't have to write a check, which gets a lot more scrutiny from the accounting team.

We can all be proud when it comes to partnerships. We want the big-dollar title sponsorship to help us pay for our racing program, but everyone has to start small. Build your program in little steps. Do your research and be willing to take product in exchange for your partnership activities rather than cash.

At this point, your sponsors are helping you with credibility as much as you help them with promotion. They are helping you build your brand and even when talking to other potential partners. Once you land that first product partnership and place their logo on the side of the car, the next partnership becomes easier as you've proven that you can be trusted by at least one brand. Build on this to continue to enhance your team's credibility.

It will feel a little like you're giving away the store at first, providing prime real estate to a product partnership and not a paid partnership. Keep in mind you have to start somewhere. In your discussions, make it clear that if a paid partner comes along, product partner branding may need to move to a different location. Most product partners will understand this.

Put a value on the product partnership. Use the retail value of the product or service. For MMB Imagery, that value was $2,500 a year. Michelle was going to retain her brand location on the car until we had a partner willing to offer us more than that in return for partnership, in cash or in product.

Your goal with that first partnership is to leverage it to draw other partners to the team. Give away more real estate than seems reasonable to that first partner. Bob's Sandwich Shop may have only given you and the team $1,000 in sandwiches for the year, but your large Bob's logo on the car will draw in others to the party. If Bob trusts you, then they should too. They have no idea what Bob paid to be the presumed title sponsor for your car.

Just like we did with Michelle and MMB, be upfront with Bob's Sandwich Shop. Let them know that you will promote them as your title sponsor and as your partnerships grow, you may need to move their branding to a less prominent location.

No one will ask you if your partners are paid or product. They will just assume that if a company has partnered with you, they're paying you. Use this to your advantage and treat all of your partnerships as if they are paid partnerships, because in essence, they are. Every dollar you don't have to spend on brake pads or tires is a dollar that goes towards funding your race program.

Some racers look down on product partnerships as lesser agreements. Don't. Really, don't. As you build your existing partnerships, you build trust with new partners. This is about managing perception. You have been trusted by X, Y, and Z, so this new partner can trust you too. Product partnerships bring credibility, strength, and breadth to your racing program. Each of these makes it easier for a new partner to say yes. The more partners you embrace early on, the stronger your brand becomes.

Let's talk about discount partnerships, which some racers tend to shy away from. Be careful. A discount partnership can often be more beneficial for the discounter than it is for the racer, so make sure that the company is one you buy from regularly.

Think of discount partnerships in the same way you think of product partnerships. You don't want a one-time 20% off kind of thing. Ask for co-promotion when working on discount partnerships. Signing with you can be as much of a benefit to their brand as it is to yours.

It's easy to let discount partnerships distract you into providing too much value for too little return. Know the amount of the sponsorship. 10% off on $1,000 is $100. Know the funding you are getting and apply the power of your brand promotion accordingly.

FROM PRODUCT TO PAID

As you sign each partner, product or otherwise, make a partnership announcement. Did you re-sign them for next year? Announce it and show them some love. From the first moment, treat product partnerships as if they are paid partnerships. Because that's what you want them to become. There is a transition step, but your goal is to convert those product partnerships into paid partnerships.

The more you treat product partnerships like paid partnerships, the more likely they will be willing to talk about taking the next step towards funding. In each part of the agreement, you need to come to the table as if they are writing you a check. Because that's exactly what you want them to do. Show them the value, overdeliver, and then have the conversation about growing your relationship into something more.

This sounds simple, but how do you actually do it?

Make sure you and your partner are getting the value you need out of the agreement. Start with your annual review and take time to overview the prior year's performance. Did you overachieve on your deliverables? Bring this data to the table. Your first goal is to extend your agreement with your current partner. Your second goal is to convert a portion to cash.

Ask for a renewal. Then ask how they would like to grow the partnership for the following year. If they ask you to do more, put a dollar figure on the additional responsibility. This will begin the conversation of converting from product to paid.

Are you using all the product they provide you? Is it too much product and a little more funding would go further? Find the compromise. You'll be surprised how often this can pivot from a product-only to a combination paid and product partnership.

Most partnerships that start out as product partnerships will always have an element of product associated with the agreement. Your job is to show so much value each year from your agreement that your partner will recognize how far above and beyond you've gone. This will help you lay out the next steps in a combination partnership.

It's ok to start out small. Keep the product support the same and ask for help with entry fees or fuel costs or some other tangible element of your program. Tell them what you spend and ask for help offsetting these expenses. It is a good starting point for any of your discussions.

It also helps them tell the story in a tangible way to their bosses. "Yes, we help them and we pay for their entry fees" is a better story than, "Yes, we help them and we give them cash too."

Giving them something specific to cover is one more way to help them justify the amount they provide you.

CONNECT YOUR PRODUCT PARTNERS

This is about seeing around corners. Connect your partners. All of them. You never know what synergies they can come up with during a race weekend brainstorm session. Now is the time to show them an additional piece of the marketing puzzle.

As you connect your partners with each other, you'll be surprised how often cross-promotion opportunities arise just from them talking to each other about how they support you in racing. Cross-promotion opportunities come about through these connections. For many partners, it is this interaction that they are seeking as they build partnerships with grassroots racers. They may want access to other partners to find new ways of promoting their product or service. Be the connector and the glue that helps them see these opportunities.

You can also ask your product partners if they know of or have additional company contacts, suppliers, or customers that would be interested in partnering with you. Don't be shy. Your current partners team with you because they support you and they like what you do for them. Having a recommendation from a partner already working with you is like having an advocate at the table.

EVALUATING BRAND COMPATIBILITY

You are working your tail off to build your portfolio of product and paid partnerships. How do you make sure that each new partner is compatible with your existing ones? The first step is simple and, at this point, you are doing it automatically as you make sure each partner fits with your brand.

As you grow your group of partners, you will need to run potential new partners by your existing ones to make sure that there aren't incompatibilities you may be unaware of. List out all of your partners when you are developing your new relationships and run new potential partners by your existing ones.

You don't need their approval necessarily, but you do need to know if they have an issue. Most contracts will stipulate that you cannot work with or promote competitive brands. This is pretty obvious. But, what if that new product partnership you're working on burned one of your other partners in a deal years ago that you had no idea about. You want to know this before you sign the contract.

You need to make the right decisions for your brand and theirs. You want 1+1 to equal three rather than minus several thousand. Let your existing partners know who you're courting. You don't have to do this until you're about to sign. Let your new partner know that the partnership is contingent on approval by existing partners. This is typically a pretty easy conversation, but don't skip it. You don't want to uncover skeletons in the race track closet. It makes for very uncomfortable conversations.

SELLING TIRES

One last thing. This is super important. Know what is in the contract you are signing. Most product partnerships will include a stipulation that you do not sell the free product they give you. Know this. It may feel like selling off unused free product is a good way to add some cash to your race funds, but you are unintentionally competing with your partner for retail sales. If a partner gives you a free asset of tires and you sell them for 50% off to somebody who would have bought them at retail, then you just cost your partner a sale. That's the opposite of what you're supposed to be doing for your partner.

If you end up with a surplus of product at the end of the year, let your partners know. Ask if you can adjust the amount for the next season. This is another good time to open the door to a product plus paid discussion.

Some companies cannot, because of their accounting rules, office politics, or whatever, give you cash even if they want to. They're totally okay with giving you product though, and will give you permission to sell the free product they gave you to help fund your racing.

If it's not clear which side your partner is on with regard to selling product, ask. Better to know than to become competition for your partner.

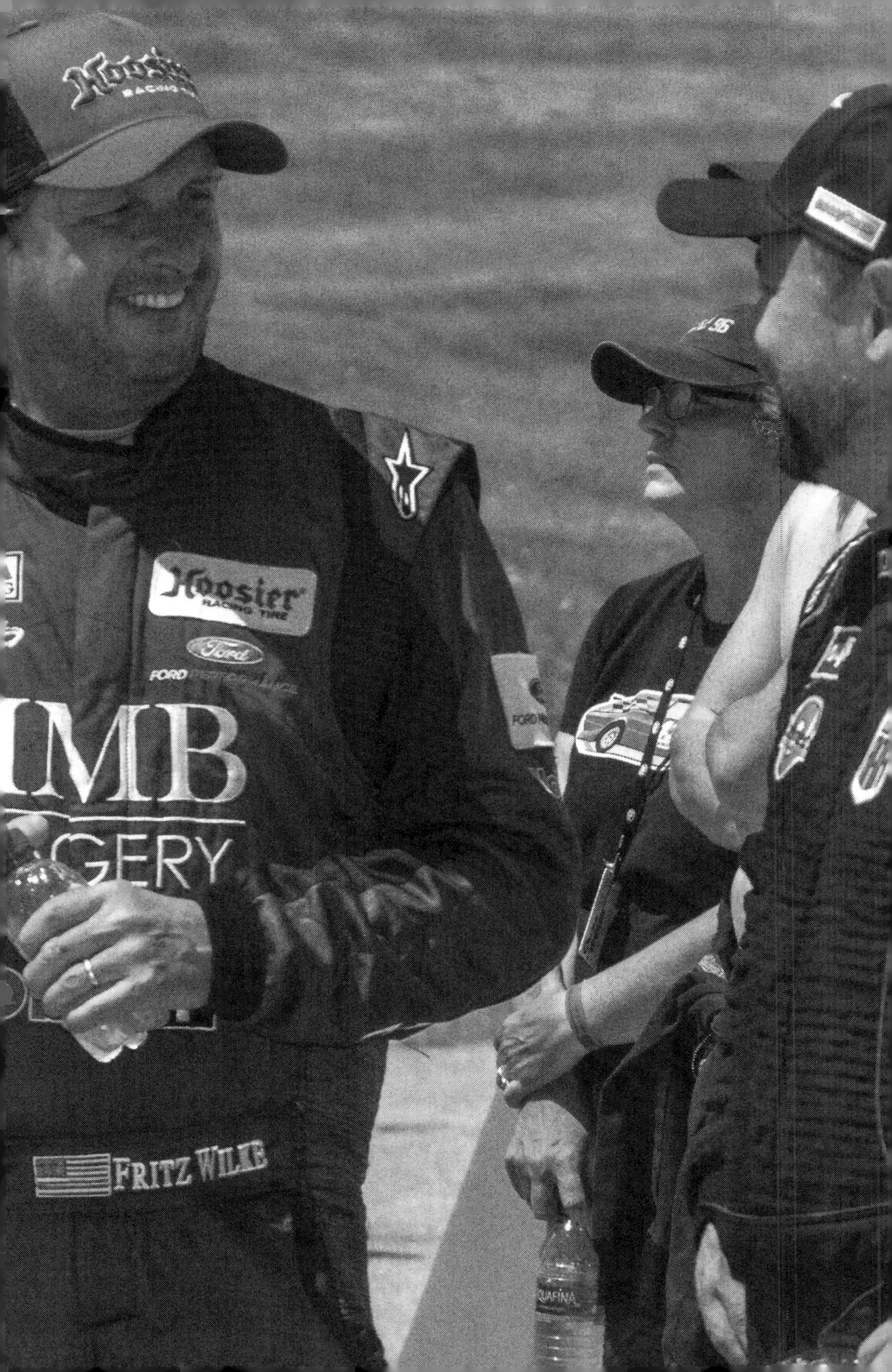
Hoosier
Hoosier
RACING TIRE
Ford
IMB
GERY
FRITZ WILKE

18

USING YOUR BRAND TO OPEN THE RIGHT DOORS

I want to close with a story from my time at Ford. I was Mustang Brand Manager and Performance and Enthusiast Marketing Manager. I was in my third year running the Ford displays at the Barrett-Jackson Auto Auction in Scottsdale.

Our display was at the entrance to the auction. Everyone who attended walked through our display. We had Ford and Lincoln cars on display in their own unique environments. We had two Mustangs on a custom-built dyno stage where customers could drag race against each other.

We arrived at Scottsdale ten days early to build our display. We put Ford signage throughout the auction space as well as multiple satellite displays, kiosks, and a ride and drive program. It was a big presence. With a display this spread out, we needed to manage our branded presence both in person and on TV.

I sat with Speed Channel Producer Rick Miner early in the week to review signage locations from each camera angle. The man knows everything about producing live TV. I learned from every interaction with him. We made sure our branding was lit properly and in the background of the most popular shots.

Once the signage was placed, we built our branded presence at the entrance. We went through dozens of meetings at Ford over several months each year to get the branded presence just right, introducing just enough change year over year to keep it fresh.

This year we had the crazy idea to build a 50-foot-high Goodwood-style sculpture above the auction entrance. We spent several weeks designing a curving and twisting spear with a Mustang convertible upside down at the tip. The Mustang would hang above the fans as they were waiting to get into the auction.

We designed this stainless-steel art piece and developed all the structural solutions to go with it. My team solved all the real-world challenges it presented. They cut their teeth designing Vegas stage shows, so this was a piece of cake. The sculpture was amazing!

Unfortunately, at the last minute, after much debate, we got cold feet and decided not to do it. Ford had just lost one billion dollars that year and we were not comfortable spending $100K on what ultimately was a very visible and very expensive piece of art.

I loved that sculpture and still wish we had done it, but there are times in business where you have to keep the bigger picture in mind. Someday, they'll do it and it will make me smile.

We still wanted to create an amazing display that week in January. A few days in, a rep for Mother's Wax approached me. A car that was supposed to be in their display was a no-show. They asked if we had any spares. I thought for a bit and asked them where they were going the rest of this year. Most of their events were on the Chevy Power Tour. That made my decision.

This unintended partnership would get our brand into a place we couldn't go with a car-care company that took immense pride in their products and presentation of the vehicles in their displays. Our car would be spotless.

I offered up one of our new GT500s, our branded signage, and wheel stand. I gave them a product specialist to train them on the features of the car. I offered them the car for the year with the stipulation that it was featured at each of their events.

I asked one more thing in return. I asked them to come to our display at Barrett-Jackson a couple of times a day in their Mother's branded gear to keep our Ford and Lincoln cars clean and free of fingerprints.

Our two brands reinforced each other. We only trusted Mother's to keep our cars clean and we got our GT500 into the Chevy Power Tour. They got a draw for their booth that was unusual in a Chevy-branded event. Sometimes, things just work out.

TELL YOUR BRAND STORY

As you grow your club racing brand, it will start to take on a soul of its own. Your brand will interact with your friends, followers, and fans just like you do. Tell your story. Help people understand who you are.

Each interaction you have with others will build your network. Take opportunities to talk about your brand, tell your story, and let people know where you are going on your racing adventure. You never know who you might run across and who may be telling your stories to others.

BE TRUE TO YOUR BRAND

Now that you've built your brand, it will be easier to connect with partners. Represent your brand in its best light and be true to your brand. You may find a potential partner that isn't quite the right fit, or maybe even a wrong fit, but they are offering up fantastic incentives. Be true to your brand here and think through your decision.

It is a lot easier to be yourself and be true to the brand you know and love than it is to try to be something you aren't. You are much more likely to make missteps when you're trying to be something somebody else wants you to be.

When you represent yourself and your brand to others, be bold, be confident, but be real. You will want to stretch the truth a little here and there. We're all bench racers, after all. Do your hardest to put your best and your real foot forward. We all can fall foul of that trap of wanting to be more when we're not quite there yet.

You *make* good things happen. They don't happen on their own. It takes a lot of hard work and a dedication to consistency and the six elements of branding to care for and feed your brand. When you interact with others, bring the passion, energy, and enthusiasm for your sport to the table.

ASK

If I can leave you with just one thing to guide you in growing partnerships that are right for you and your brand it is this: ask your partners what they need from you before you tell them what else you can do. Asking this question every three to four months will build your relationship.

As you continue to grow your brand, check in frequently with your partners to make sure their needs haven't changed. Is there anything new on the horizon that they need your help with? Do they have a new product launch that needs support, a new business focus, or a new market they're going after? You just have to ask. Make sure you share things you are doing for your other partners and see if any of those ideas can help.

In the end, be the best partner you can be, overdeliver, and keep them updated. You got this.

CLOSING THOUGHTS

You can do this. It really comes down to that belief. It takes insight, some perseverance, a willingness to make mistakes and learn from them quickly, a desire for consistency, and a dedication to staying true to the brand that you created. As you take this journey, you will come to stumbling blocks and places where it seemed like there was no clear answer on what to do next or how to do it.

Keep moving forward. Try, fail, and adjust. Repeat over and over and over until you look forward to that next failure so you can continue to learn and grow your brand. Soon, you'll be able to take what you learned about branding in this book and apply it to your club racing program and watch as it grows and blossoms.

A brand needs care and feeding, and will stagnate and die if left alone for too long. You are the one who will help keep your brand growing. Care for your brand, grow it, and lean on it to enhance the reach of your club racing program no matter what series you race in. Most of all, stay in touch with your partners, friends, fans, and followers. They are the glue. Bring them along on your journey.

As I finish this section, something Carroll Shelby—may God rest his soul—said to me once at a dinner still rings true. I was telling him about our adventures ice racing Shelby Omnis in the 90s.

"You should've called me," he said. "I would have helped you."

"You don't just pick up the phone and call Carroll Shelby," I replied. He looked at me for a moment.

"Well," he said in that familiar, matter of fact tone, "if you had a pair of balls you would have." He said it with that grin of his and that twinkle in his eye that let me know he was equal parts serious and teasing.

That conversation in Tulsa, Oklahoma, one of many we had over the years, comes back to me from time to time. Be brave and be bold. Ask for help from anyone you think will help you. You'll be surprised where the best help will come from. The big personalities often have the biggest hearts and we all remember where we came from and want to help the next generation succeed. In many ways, that's why this book exists.

Have fun on your branding adventure. It's a lot to take in at once, but as you put the pieces in place and use the six elements of branding to build and nurture a strong brand, pretty soon you'll step back and smile with pride at this brand that you've brought to life. Good luck and go get 'em!

READING LIST

Motorsports Marketing and Sponsorships: How to Raise Money to Race and Give Sponsors What They Really Want by Alex Striller

Get The Drive: The Only Way to Get Motorsports Sponsorship Now by Enzo Mucci

Where the Writer Meets the Road by Sam Posey

Start With Why by Simon Sinek

Dirty Little Secrets of Buzz by David Seaman

The Last Open Road by Burt Levy

Life in the Fast Lane by Steve Matchett

Go Faster! Mastering the Art of Race Driving by Skip Barber Racing School

PHOTOGRAPHY RESOURCES

Michael Berchak. Trackside Photography. BerchakMedia.com

Joseph Bierschbach. Trackside Photography. RedCasePhotography@gmail.com

Rob Bodle. Trackside Photography. Rob-Bodle.com

Alex Conley. Video. ACMDetroit.com

Rick Corwine. Trackside Photography. Rickcorwine.smugmug.com

Dave Green. Trackside Photography. Flagtoflagphotography.com

Jeff Loewe. Trackside photography. Jlofoto.net jloewe@cinci.rr.com

Michelle Massey Barnes. Portrait Photography. MMBImagery.com

John Pringle. Trackside Photography. JPringleMedia@gmail.com

John Sukowaty. Trackside Photography and Video. RacedayPhotog.com john@skwty.com

Fritz Wilke. Fritzwilke.com Fritz@fritzwilke.com

FRITZ WILKE RACING PARTNERS

MMB Imagery
Frozen Rotors
Hawk Performance
Hoosier Racing Tire
Racers360
Mobil 1
Stilo USA
Noah Stark Engine Works
Performance Motorsports Network
Central Coast Solutions
Chimney Mechanix
PKT Axles
BTCC Blueprints
Capaldi Racing
Optima Batteries
Ink Frenzy

THE NEXT STEP

As you walk through this book, if you find that you need help or clarification, please feel free to reach out. I'm happy to assist you on your branding journey in any way I can. I also offer individualized racing brand consulting services through Fritz Wilke Racing. We're all club racers and that's what club racers do—help each other get better and faster. You can reach me at fritz@fritzwilke.com.

ACKNOWLEDGEMENTS

Thank you to Will for your determination and passion for karting. You are an inspiration to me every day. Thank you to Kristine for your unlimited patience with me on this project and the time I take to go on racing adventures. I'm so glad we're on this journey together!

Thank you to my book coach, Rebecca Zornow, from Conquer Books for your constant help through this process. Thank you to Terra L. Fletcher for your inspiration and willingness to help me get back going on this project. Thank you to my teammate and partner in crime, Jasper Drengler, for being the most resilient human being I have ever known and for showing me that there is always a way forward.

Thank you to my Mayhem Racing friends - Mark and Mary Utecht, Joe and Trina Huttle, Wade Roggemann, Jay and Carolyn Luehmann for teaching me about club racing.

Thank you to my Capaldi Racing friends—Alex Perales, Leo, Sandie and Craig Capaldi, Dave Marchione and the rest of the team—even Radar—for teaching me how a pro team does things in club racing. Your professionalism set the standard by which I judge our performance year over year.

Thank you to Alex Striller, Matt Martelli, Vaughn Gittin Jr., Tommy Kendall, Nick Fousekis, Tanner Foust, and Scott Pruett for all the time you took talking with me over the years. You may not have known it, but all of you influenced me and inspired me to write this book.

Thank you to Michael Berchak, Joseph Bierschbach, Rob Bodle, Alex Conley, Rick Corwine, Dave Green, Jeff Loewe, Michelle Massey Barnes, John Pringle, and John Sukowaty for all of your passion and dedication to our sport. I appreciate you standing in the hot sun, creating your art and capturing memories for all of us club racers.

Thank you to Jost Capito, Jim Farley, Robert Parker, Vivian Palmer, Theo Benson, and Paul Anderson for your guidance and mentorship during my time at Ford and Ford Performance. It had its ups and downs for sure, but I had some amazing experiences that I wouldn't trade for anything. I learned what it means to be a world-class marketer and leader from each of you.

PHOTOGRAPHY CREDITS

Front Cover: Rick Corwine. Road America Turn Six
Dedication: Michelle Massey Barnes. Hero Card
Contents: Jeff Loewe. Indy Pagoda

Part I: Fritz Wilke. Helmet at Sebring
Part II: Rob Bodle. Sebring Hairpin
Part III: Rob Bodle. VIR 5
Part IV: Michael Berchak. Miatas

Chapter 1: Jeff Loewe. Gloves
Chapter 2: Jeff Loewe. VIR Lower Esses
Chapter 3.1: Michael Berchak. Mid O Spec Racer Fords
Chapter 3.2: Pat Doyle. Brainerd Turn six
Chapter 4: John Sukowaty. Road America – the view from the hill at five
Chapter 5.1: Michelle Massey Barnes. Jim at Indy
Chapter 5.2: Dave Green. Turn One Sebring
Chapter 6: John Pringle. Grattan Testing
Chapter 7: John Sukowaty. Speedville Bridge
Chapter 8: Michael Berchak. Mid-O Miatas
Chapter 9: John Sukowaty. Fan Deck Road America
Chapter 10.1: Michelle Massey Barnes. On the Fence
Chapter 10.2: Jeff Loewe. Fiesta Roof
Chapter 11.1: Michael Berchak. PittRace Front Straight
Chapter 11.2: Fritz Wilke. VIR Paddock
Chapter 12: Fritz Wilke. Driver in Car
Chapter 13: Michael Berchak. VIR lower Esses
Chapter 14.1: Michelle Massey Barnes. Team and Pagoda
Chapter 14.2: Jeff Loewe. Fiesta Wheel
Chapter 15: John Sukowaty. Road America – the view from Canada
Chapter 16: Jeff Loewe. Road Atlanta Turn 9
Chapter 17: Michelle Massey Barnes. GingerMan 2017
Chapter 18.1: Michael Berchak. Mid-Ohio Tower
Chapter 18.2: Jeff Loewe. June Sprints

Closing Thoughts: Rob Bodle. VIR Esses
Closing Thoughts: Michelle Massey Barnes. Indy with Will
Reading List: Rob Bodle. VIR Oaktree
Reading List: Jeff Loewe. June Sprints Start
Fritz Wilke Racing Partners: Michael Berchak. PittRace
Next Steps: Jeff Loewe. VIR
Acknowledgements: Joseph Bierschbach COTA
Photography Credits: Fritz Wilke. Grid at USAir Motorsports Park
About the Author: Michelle Massey Barnes
Inside Back Cover: Jeff Loewe. PittRace

227

ABOUT THE AUTHOR

FRITZ WILKE is a marketer, storyteller, brand ambassador, author, and public speaker. Fritz grew up in Indiana with the sounds of the Indy 500 broadcast igniting his passion for motorsports. He is a former Fortune 500 marketer and long-time front-runner in the Sports Car Club of America's premier national amateur road racing series, the Hoosier Super Tour.

Fritz honed his marketing skills at Ford Motor Company. Over his decade-plus experience with the company he has held roles as Mustang Brand Manager, Event and Enthusiast Marketing Manager, Ford Performance Product Marketing Manager, and more.

Fritz is the founder of Fritz Wilke Racing and Ollie Rocket Racing. He is co-founder along with Jasper Drengler of the Flying Ghost Racing Team. When Fritz isn't racing, he's helping others market their racing teams and build their partnership programs. He's also crew chief for his son Will, who's competing in the Cup Kart North America national karting series.

Printed in Poland
by Amazon Fulfillment
Poland Sp. z o.o., Wrocław